THE AMERICAN
MAN'S GARDEN

THE AMERICAN MAN'S GARDEN

ROSEMARY VEREY

IN ASSOCIATION WITH KATHERINE LAMBERT

Foreword by Allen Lacy

A BULFINCH PRESS BOOK

Little, Brown and Company · Boston · Toronto · London

To Kevin Nicolay, artist and gardener,

who sadly did not live to see its publication,

this book is affectionately dedicated.

BAS-TITLE: *Helleborus orientalis,* selected 'black', from Helen Ballard, from the garden of Kevin Nicolay.
TITLE PAGE: An 1860s Delaware springhouse is a principal feature of the garden of William H. Frederick, Jr.

FIRST EDITION

Library of Congress Cataloging-in-Publication Data

Verey, Rosemary.
    The American man's garden / by Rosemary Verey in association with
Katherine Lambert; foreword by Allen Lacy. — 1st ed.
        p.   cm.
    ISBN 0-8212-1774-7
        1. Gardens — United States.   2. Gardens — Canada.   3. Gardeners —
United States.   4. Gardeners — Canada.   5. Landscape gardening —
United States.   6. Landscape gardening — Canada.   I. Lambert,
Katherine.   II. Title.
    SB466.U6V46 1990
    712'.097 — dc20   90-34294
                                                                CIP

Bulfinch Press is an imprint and trademark of Little, Brown and Company (Inc.)
Published simultaneously in Canada by Little, Brown & Company (Canada) Limited

PRINTED IN SINGAPORE

CONTENTS

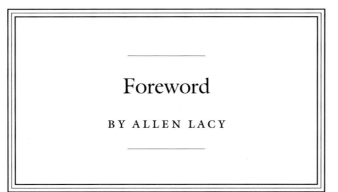
WITH THE AMERICAN MAN'S GARDEN, Rosemary Verey rounds out a quintet of books in which some 155 gardeners in the English-speaking world, of both sexes and on both sides of the Atlantic Ocean, describe in very personal and loving terms the gardens they have made for their own delight and for the pleasure of others. Taken together, *The Englishwoman's Garden, The New Englishwoman's Garden, The Englishman's Garden* (all written with Alvilde Lees-Milne), *The American Woman's Garden* (written with Ellen Samuels), and now this final and very handsome book in the series offer a detailed picture of horticulture as it flourishes in the United States as well as in Great Britain in the last decades of the twentieth century. The format developed for the first volume in the series, *The Englishwoman's Garden,* has proved sound. Although the lavish color photographs show these many gardens as they appear to the quasi-objective eye of the camera, the words describing them come from the gardeners themselves. To read these books is to eavesdrop on a great and animated conversation in which some very dedicated gardeners speak passionately about their love of plants—in some cases a love of long standing in their lives, in others a love that overcame them fairly recently.

The two books on American gardens are particularly useful in correcting the false notion that many Americans have about our horticulture's being vastly inferior to that of Great Britain. Except for some fine public gardens in the United States—notably Longwood, Winterthur, Wave Hill, and Filoli—our gardens are largely private. They are not open to the general public, although a passing stranger who tells a gardener that he likes what he can see from the sidewalk will often be invited to come inside for a closer look. Great Britain has its private gardens as well, but the realities of taxation in the years since World War II have transformed many private gardens into public ones owned by the National Trust. I have visited Sissinghurst Castle and many other showplaces of British horticulture by paying admission. Before the end of the war, I doubt that I would have had a chance to glory in the genius of Vita Sackville-West and the garden she made there; all the evidence suggests that she treasured her privacy. The result of these changes is that American tourists who are interested in gardening now return from Great Britain somewhat overwhelmed by the gardens that they can see so easily there. (This accessibility has been increased by the National Gardens Scheme, by which many fine private gardens are open to the public at least one or two days a year.) Since many of the best American gardens remain invisible to us, we tend to make invidious and unwarranted comparisons with British examples. We may also be tempted to use plants that are well suited to the gentle and lingering British summer—meconopsis, for instance—but will not survive our own hot weather from June to mid-August.

A woodland path lined with hostas in the Vermont garden of Joe Eck and Wayne Winterrowd.

In autumn the crape myrtle (*Lagerstroemia indica* 'Potomac') provides an element of drama in the small town plot in Virginia where Phillip Watson has made a garden that is full of interest throughout the year.

The American Woman's Garden and now *The American Man's Garden* provide a valuable and proper perspective on the possibilities of the gardening enterprise in many parts of our country. Indeed, the books successfully capture one of the signal features of gardening in America: a diversity so enormous that it makes generalizations far more difficult than is the case for British gardening. We garden over ten winter-hardiness zones, ranging from areas where frost is virtually unknown to regions where winters are long and brutal. Southerners also have to take into account the seldom-discussed question of summer hardiness—the ability of plants to withstand hot and humid nights over a period of two months or more. Soils vary dramatically as well. New England is predominantly blessed (or cursed) with soil whose main crop sometimes seems to be rocks. The Atlantic coastal plain has its sandy loams, Georgia and the Carolina piedmont their red clays, Texas its black gumbo soils, and the Southwest its adobes and caliches. The soil is acidic in some parts of the country, alkaline in others. The amount of annual rainfall—and its distribution within the year—varies staggeringly from place to place. Our native flora is also highly differentiated: people who are reared in Maine and visit southern Florida for the first time, for example, will be bewildered, knowing neither the common nor the scientific names of most of the plants growing in gardens or along the roadsides.

This diversity supplies a quite satisfactory answer to the obvious question: why should an Englishwoman edit a pair of books on American gardens? Rosemary Verey, as an outsider with a strong interest in the state of our horticulture, sees more clearly than an American could all the differences that divide us; even gardeners who have lived in many locations in America tend to judge by their most recent setting and experience. (I was startled a September or two ago when a friend in Texas wrote to me about planting her second crop of tomatoes. Although I grew up in Dallas and made my first garden there before I was ten, some forty-five years ago, I had forgotten that Texans plant tomatoes twice a year.)

I confess that when I got the manuscript of *The American Man's Garden* I first reread *The American Woman's Garden*, out of simple curiosity. Would there be patterns involving differences of gender? Are some gardens "masculine" and others "feminine," or would I find something like the arrangement at Sissinghurst whereby Harold Nicolson provided the eye for design and Vita Sackville-West the eye for plants? If there are any such patterns of difference here, they have eluded me. I would not know what to look for in a garden to determine whether it was made by a male or by a female. And indeed, this new book, about the gardens that men in our country have created and held high in their affections, underlines a point often made by Wendell Berry, one of our clearest thinkers: males, as well as females, may be nurturers—nurturers of both plants and people.

And no matter what the reader's gender may be, *The American Man's Garden* has much to teach about plants that are worth trying, about particularly successful combinations of plants, and about what the late Elizabeth Lawrence called "gardening for love."

Acknowledgments

I COULD NOT HAVE CONSIDERED editing this book had it not been for the generous hospitality shown to me over the last ten years and the wonderful kindness with which friends have allowed me to see their gardens and taken me to visit others all over America. I have learned much about the history and the making of American gardens and have had the privilege of being shown private gardens by their owners, and historic gardens and others by famous landscape designers. During these years the interest in gardening has increased in America to such an extent that it is now among the most popular leisure pursuits.

My special thanks go to the people with whom I have stayed: Ollie Adams, Marilyn Alaimo, Paul and Joan Arbon, Byrd and Bourne Bean, Zinkie Benton, Frank and Anne Cabot, Bessie and Robert Carter, Mary Wayne Dixon, Susan Dulany, Charlie and Mary Gale, Chuck and Barbara Gale, Penny Harris, Kathy Hendricks, Barbara Keightle, Peg Keller, Mary Lou and Spencer Kellogg, Fenton and Libba Keyes, Bill and Janet Klein, Sally Lee, Richard Lewis and Susan de Rose, Sarah Logan, Elizabeth Manners, Lyndon Miller, Rose Monroe, Cynthia Nolan, Jane Pepper, Kathy Pitney, Nancy Power, Betty Rollins, Chris Rosmini, Sandra Ross, Tobe Rothaus, Ellen Samuels, Christine Schmidt, Holly Shimizu, Holt and Isabel Souder, Mimi Stockwell, Rose Strachan, Marco Polo Stufano, Peg Washington, Sarah and Virginia Weatherly, Eleanor Weller, Carolyn Weston, Gene White, Tata White, Sue Whitsun, Elizabeth Woodburn, and Tom Woodham.

Others have shown me around their own gardens or have given advice and shared their knowledge with me: Marty Adams, Georgia Adler, Louisa Allen, Garland and Mary Anderson, Caroline Benson, Susie Blair, Betty Bogart, Susan Botts, Douna Bowman, Betty Brown, Kathy Buchanan, Mrs. Cason Callaway, Anne Carr, Lena Carron, Mrs. Thomas Church, Madeline Davidson, Michael Dirr, Charles Duell, Linda Emmick, Barry Ferguson, Jenny Fitch, Timmie Gallagher, Charmaine Giuliana, Drayton Hastie, Peter Hatch, Mrs. Lyndon B. Johnson, John Koros, Virginia Louisell, Mimi Lyon, Elizabeth McLean, Fred and Mary Ann McGourty, Susan Marcus, Augusta Maynard, David Northington, Hal Northrup, Dean Norton, Ben Page, Dick Page, Margaret Parke, Wendy Powell, Peggy Rockefeller, Betty Scholtz, Bill and Erika Shanks, Trudy Stamper, Joan Stein, Beth Straus, Kathleen Summerall, Jane Symmes, Tim Tomlinson, Shelley Wanger, Olive and George Waters, Charles Webster, Emily Whaley, Lynne White, Pat Wilson, Louisa Farrand Wood, Dorothy Woods, and Mrs. St. Clair Wright.

Visitors to my own garden have been patient with my requests for advice. They include Donald Olson and Cliff Widerski, Leonard Perry, and Rob Proctor.

My particular thanks go to Tony Lord, formerly gardens adviser to the National Trust in England, now a free-lance horticultural consultant, for the invaluable help he has given me with nomenclature.

Katherine Lambert has been the essential friend and fellow editor in this book. She has typed and telephoned, coordinated with Betty Childs and the contributors, and above all kept me up to date.

Finally, I am grateful to the designer, Susan Marsh, and at Bulfinch Press, the copyeditor, Dorothy Straight, the production coordinator, Christina Holz Eckerson, and most of all my editor, Betty Childs.

R. V.

Robert Dash, an artist living, painting, and gardening on Long Island, makes vivid and unusual use of color: here, bright-yellow railings, their shapes echoing the stripped "ballerina" trunks of his privet hedge.

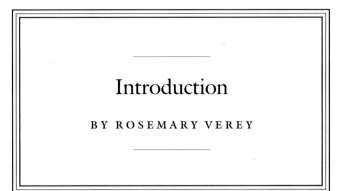

Introduction

BY ROSEMARY VEREY

THE MEN WHOSE GARDENS APPEAR in this book are working in a long tradition. Owners of large estates and small gardens, botanists and plant collectors, and professional designers and landscape architects have all contributed to the development of the American garden over the last four centuries.

Man and his garden have always been interdependent: his garden reflects what he lacks in his immediate environment. Surrounded by genuine wilderness, the settlers arriving from Europe in the seventeenth century wanted security and order in their gardens. Fences kept out livestock, and a formal design of straight rows and paths made these plots productive and easy to maintain. They reflected the gardens of Elizabethan England but went beyond them in their use of native materials. Yet even in those early years, a garden was a haven as well as a necessity: John Winthrop, Jr., son of the first governor of Massachusetts, noted with pleasure "stepping out into [his] garden."

The settlers brought gardening books with them. Two of the most important were John Parkinson's *Paradisi in Sole* (1629) and Leonard Meager's *English Gardener* (1676). Parkinson gave a verbal description of the shape of an ideal garden, with arbors for shade and rest, knots and hedges. John Winthrop III had a copy of Meager's book, which was so popular in England that it ran to six printings. It is supremely practical, less sophisticated than Parkinson's work. I can imagine how much the plain directions, descriptions of herbs and flowers, and designs for formal layouts would have appealed to the seventeenth-century New England gardeners.

John Josselyn, author of *New-Englands Rarities* (1672) and *Account of Two Voyages to New England* (1673), gives much information regarding plants and tools. He tells of beds made especially for tobacco seedlings—real flower "beds," long and narrow and raised above ground level (like beds for people) and so much easier to care for than ordinary flat plots. His account is reminiscent of the writings of Thomas Hill and William Lawson, whose books the settlers would also have carried with them from England.

It was the women, in fact, who tended the grounds around the homestead, while the men had the heavy task of taming the land. But the men too were soon contributing to the gardens by collecting unknown and interesting plants on their forays into the wild, bringing them home to be cultivated in the areas around their dwellings. The women must have been delighted!

Plant and seed collection increased, and the development and horticultural interest of the gardens was greatly enhanced by the eighteenth-century spirit of curiosity. A lively communication began between the gardeners of the New World and the Old. Early in the century, Mark Catesby (better known for his paintings and studies of

A dramatic planting of white digitalis and deep-blue anchusa in Sir John Thouron's garden, influenced by the owner's Scottish roots but set against a backdrop of serene Pennsylvania countryside.

George Washington's formal vegetable garden at Mount Vernon reflects his knowledge of the eighteenth-century French and English potager as well as the grace of the American colonial age.

natural history) arrived from England, sponsored by the Royal Society, and sent seeds home to Bishop Compton in London. Similarly, James Oglethorpe, founder of Georgia, shipped plants and seeds from that area to Philip Miller at the Chelsea Physic Garden in London and received shipments in return. Miller's *Gardeners Dictionary*, of 1731, the first comprehensive reference book of its kind, was so well known on both sides of the Atlantic that it was used as a mail-order reference in describing plants and seeds.

The amazing father and son John and William Bartram collected seeds and plants extensively on the East Coast, and their discoveries changed the face of many gardens, both in America and in England. John Bartram corresponded with the English botanist Peter Collinson for thirty-three years, beginning in 1735. He sent consignments of seeds and plants to England for Collinson to distribute, mostly to aristocrats with large estates, each of whom paid a subscription of £5 for a box of horticultural treasures. (Today you can visit John Bartram's twenty-seven-acre garden on the Schuylkill River near Philadelphia, where many of the plants that he and his son collected still grow.)

As in England, gardening was a legitimate gentleman's hobby, combining beauty with elegance, utility, and good husbandry. George Washington wrote to Alexander Spotswood in 1788, "I think with you that the life of a Husbandman of all others is the most delectable. It is honorable. It is amusing, and, with judicious management, it is profitable."

Washington inherited Mount Vernon in 1754, creating his garden on a site overlooking the Potomac River. It is a magnificent setting, a perfect example of Charles Sprague Sargent's later advice to gardeners to make the plan fit the ground, not to twist the ground to fit the plan. A Polish visitor described the property in 1798:

> It is well cultivated, perfectly kept, and is quite in English style. . . .
> The whole plantation, the garden, and the rest prove well that a man
> born with natural taste may guess a beauty without having ever seen
> its model. The General has never left America; but when one sees his
> house and his home and his garden it seems as if he had copied the
> best samples of the grand old homesteads of England.

Formal planting is perfectly adapted to incorporate the ideas Washington drew from literature on the English landscape movement—he even included a ha-ha, first used at Rousham in Oxfordshire. In the English fashion, the southeast facade of the house looks down a well-timbered parkland sloping toward the river.

During his frequent absences from Mount Vernon, Washington kept in close touch with his manager. Through letters of instruction, accounts, plans, and plant lists, we become aware of his gardening interests, especially his love of trees. He wanted groves without order or regularity, using "the clever kind of trees," especially flowering ones: magnolias with scented flowers and liriodendrons with flowers like tulips. The borders and paths were defined by box edging—in the garden today, boxwood is a principal feature.

The garden at Mount Vernon was restored in the 1930s to Washington's original plans and planting, and recent restoration has made it even more accurate. During his tenure it was much visited; he himself said, "I have no objection to any sober or orderly person's gratifying their curiosity in viewing the buildings, Gardens &tc about Mount Vernon." Today it receives many thousands of visitors annually.

Like Washington, Thomas Jefferson loved trees. He favored them in informal clumps, and he also created a grove of ornamental specimens. "My house," he said, "is entirely embosomed in high plane-trees, with good grass below; and under them I breakfast, dine, write, read and receive my company. What would I not give that the trees planted nearest round the house at Monticello were full grown." He would be happy with the mature trees that surround it now.

Jefferson lived at Monticello from 1770 until his death, in 1826. In 1786, while serving in Paris as minister to France, he visited England, studying the landscape and romantic gardens that united the surroundings of the house, the park, and the countryside. This was the style that inspired him and that he adapted to his hilltop in Virginia, with its extensive views over the rolling Piedmont landscape.

Propagating and planting traditional cottage-garden flowers, indigenous woodland flora, and exotics were Jefferson's passion, resulting in intensive groupings of bulbs, herbaceous flowers, and annuals. These are still grown at Monticello, and a new nursery has been set up to make them available to visitors. Jefferson would have approved of this, as he too carried on the tradition of botanical exchange.

William Paca, Jefferson's contemporary and also a signer of the Declaration of Independence, built a town house with a magnificent garden in Annapolis in 1763. The garden was subsequently lost, buried beneath a large hotel and a parking lot until 1965. Since then a remarkable restoration has taken place. The parterre gardens have been recreated on descending levels, and once more the white Chinese Chippendale bridge leads over the pond and into the wilderness.

Paca had been to England, and in any case he must have been aware of the prototype of his garden shown in William Lawson's book *A New Orchard & Garden*. Where Lawson had his knot garden and the river, Paca had a pool and wilderness beyond. The wilderness had become fashionable in England in the eighteenth century thanks to books by Stephen Switzer and Batty Langley, and Paca was undoubtedly influenced by them. Another influence, certainly, was William Chambers, who introduced the Chinese style to England, especially through his work at Kew.

It is tantalizing to think of other lost eighteenth-century gardens that may have been of this quality. Bacon's Castle in Surry County, Virginia, is one example; fortunately it is now in the process of being reconstructed. Will these important garden restorations have an influence on present-day designers?

Whenever gardening becomes an important hobby, nurseries spring up. By 1737 the Prince Nursery in Flushing, New York—the first to have mail-order sales—was advertising ornamental shrubs, perennials, and fruit trees. At the end of the eighteenth century, Bernard McMahon started his nursery in Philadelphia. Jefferson bought plants from both, and Washington ordered trees and shrubs from John Bartram's garden. The catalogues of these three nurseries give us an insight into the available and popular plants of the day. (Ann Leighton's book *American Gardens in the Eighteenth Century* [1970] is an interesting source on this.)

It is not surprising that in the cold-winter climate of much of the East Coast, exotics were housed in orangeries. By 1790 Charles Ridgley at Hampton in Maryland had established piped under-floor water heating in his orangery, where he cultivated oranges, lemons, and other exotics. Charles Carroll of Mount Claire, Baltimore, sent boxes of plants to George Washington for the greenhouse he had built in 1785 fronting on his flower garden.

Because of the very size of America, and its consequent huge variations in climate, each garden designer and owner has been confronted with different problems, requiring

At the Paca House, in Annapolis, the garden created in the mid–eighteenth century by William Paca on three descending levels has recently been faithfully reconstructed, based on a depiction of it in the background of a portrait of its owner.

An aerial view of the grand plantation garden at Middleton Place, South Carolina, shows the grassy "bridge" flanked by the famous butterfly-wing lakes leading to the landing stage on the Ashley River.

different approaches and materials. Two of the most interesting southern gardens, both open to the public, are in South Carolina, where the winters are reliably frost-free. Magnolia-on-the-Ashley was established as a rice plantation in the seventeenth century, with a garden of formal design. In 1836, when John Grimke Drayton inherited the property, he proclaimed his wish to create here "an earthly paradise and a soft natural beauty." He swept away the formal lines in favor of a more naturalistic design. He introduced the *Azalea indica* to America and was one of the first gardeners to use *Camellia japonica* in an outdoor setting. Today there are huge specimen trees, live oak (*Quercus virginiana*) festooned with Spanish moss, magnolias, tea olives (*Osmanthus fragrans*), and broadleaf Japanese hollies (*Ilex latifolia*).

Middleton Place is only four miles from Magnolia. Gardens grow up where the social and economic climate is favorable, and both properties were plantations that made their owners wealthy. Doris M. Stone (in *The Great Public Gardens of the Eastern United States* [1982]) contrasts the two: "Whereas Magnolia has soft feminine charm, Middleton has masculine elegance." Henry Middleton had finished laying out his garden by 1755. Guests arrived by boat up the Ashley River, and their first sight was of the grassy "bridge" leading to the house, with spectacular butterfly-wing lakes on each side.

Compared to many other formally designed gardens of that era—the Paca garden or that of the Governor's Palace in Williamsburg—Middleton Place was outstanding for its ambitious scale. It was the first American garden to be landscaped, although it also included areas of formal layout.

These two southern gardens are wonderful spectacles, as well as lessons in history. If their scale is not generally applicable to late-twentieth-century gardens, the individual plantings offer plenty of ideas.

The same is true of two great gardens farther north: Longwood, in Pennsylvania, and Winterthur, nearby in Delaware. The climate, with winter freeze and snow cover, is harsher than South Carolina's, so the variety of plants is very different. The creators of these gardens, Pierre Samuel du Pont of Longwood and Henry Francis du Pont of Winterthur, were second cousins, both great-grandsons of E. I. du Pont, a keen botanist and horticulturist who founded the Du Pont chemical company. The gardens, though only a few miles apart, reflect the different characters of their owners.

Pierre Samuel (1870–1964) was an industrial wizard and a knowledgeable gardener. In 1906 he bought Pierce's Park, where a century earlier Joshua and Samuel Pierce had begun planting a collection of ornamental trees. It was this arboretum, then maturing, that inspired Pierre to acquire the property, at the time threatened with destruction; it is now part of the 1,051 acres of Longwood Gardens.

Pierre was closely involved with the designing of his garden, though he was generally more interested in the whole concept than in the detail. Gardening he considered an event, so gardens should be designed for entertaining: the paths must be wide and straight, the water displays dramatic, and the planting bold. And he worked on a large scale: by 1921 his greenhouses covered fourteen acres.

Longwood is indeed a spectacle. Open in Pierre's time on weekends, the garden is now open every day, with outstanding displays indoors and out. Its foremost influence on American horticulture is through its educational programs.

Henry Francis du Pont, who died in 1969, inherited Winterthur from his father in 1927. Even as it exists today, Winterthur is essentially his personal creation. He loved his garden, always maintaining that he was the head gardener, and his gang of gardeners respected his well-considered ideas. He liked experimentation and innovation; he saw and absorbed both the whole effect and the detail.

Henry Francis considered that the planting and designing of his garden and the decorating of his house should be complementary, the planting outside echoing the decor within. Indeed, as one looks out of the windows at Winterthur, the paths seem to lead right into the room. Colors are coordinated. A room with sienese-yellow wallpaper and curtains looks out on dogwoods, corylopsis, and witch hazel. The striped material on the seat of a chair under a window echoes the straight trunks of three tulip trees and an American beech outside. Henry Francis was surely a most thoughtful man.

Since 1952, both house and garden have been open to the public on a regular basis. Hal Bruce, as curator of the garden, carried on du Pont's imaginative work in this sixty-acre naturalistic woodland setting until his recent death.

Quite different from the du Ponts in character and approach, but like them rich enough to indulge his fantasies, Harvey S. Ladew started planting a twenty-two-acre garden in Maryland in 1922. Talented and energetic, he designed his garden without professional help. By the time of his death, in 1976, Ladew had created the most outstanding topiary garden in America, in which his passion for fox hunting is immortalized. In his wide-ranging enthusiasm he designed fifteen gardens, each with a

From the formal pool at Winterthur, in Delaware, stone steps lead up to the house.

different theme, varying from a rose garden, a waterlily garden, and a berry garden to a wild garden growing native ferns and field flowers. They are full of ideas, both for design and for special planting.

These gardeners were all wealthy and influential men of affairs, amateur horticulturalists for whom garden making was a passionate hobby. In St. Louis in the nineteenth century, Henry Shaw, also an amateur but with a different approach, made a lasting contribution to botanical and horticultural science. A man of acquired wealth, he traveled throughout America and Europe, visiting Kew with an introduction to its director, Dr. William Hooker, and attending the Great Exhibition at Crystal Palace. Back home in St. Louis, he determined to create a park for exotic trees and plants, and in 1859—influenced by his visit to Kew—he established in that city the first American botanical garden devoted to living plants and scientific research. Henry Shaw died in 1889; now, more than a hundred years later, he would be delighted to walk in the Missouri Botanic Garden's Climatron and to see the desert house and the authentic Japanese garden.

In my mind Charles Sprague Sargent and the Arnold Arboretum in Boston are synonymous. In 1872 Sargent, a rich young man, was appointed professor of horticulture at Harvard and curator of the university's new arboretum, where he had the good fortune to work with Asa Gray, the famous botany professor. Sargent's ambition was to grow every tree and shrub from the world over that would survive the Boston winter. Ten years after Sargent was appointed, Frederick Law Olmsted, then designing the Boston parks system, began landscaping the Arboretum. Working together, Sargent and Olmsted achieved a magnificent combination of landscaping and arboriculture.

Alongside the horticulturists and the gifted and wealthy amateurs, a new group of professionals was emerging. In 1824 André Parmentier emigrated to New York and became America's first commercial landscape gardener. In his informal designs he was the forerunner of the widely influential Andrew Jackson Downing. A designer of

At the eighteenth-century Mission House in Stockbridge, Massachusetts, Fletcher Steele's design (1926–1932) reflects the formality of fruit and vegetable gardens of the colonial era.

gardens and woodlands as well as an international authority on pomology, Downing published the first American book on landscape gardening in 1841 (*A Treatise on the Theory and Practice of Landscape Gardening, Adapted to North America*). His promotion of naturalized settings was to have a lasting effect on the domestic landscape of America throughout the nineteenth century. Downing's work, cut short by his premature death, in 1852, also encouraged the creation of public gardens and influenced Frederick Law Olmsted. In 1857 Olmsted submitted the winning entry in the competition for the design of eighty-eight acres in the heart of Manhattan; since then Central Park has been a prototype for urban parks.

Despite the remarkable contributions of Downing, and later of Olmsted, the landscape field lacked widespread patronage until the last years of the nineteenth century. The Columbian Exposition of 1893, in Chicago, "proved a milestone for the young profession," writes Robin Karson (in *Fletcher Steele, Landscape Architect* [1989]). In Olmsted's scheme for the exposition, the "thoughtful disposition of buildings, inspired placement of sculpture, and poetic and lavish use of water opened the public's eyes to new possibilities in their dismal cities and around their homes."

Fletcher Steele was a link between the old style and the new, and was considered by some to be the best designer working on the East Coast during the 1920s and '30s. His influential gardens were mainly located in New York State and southern New England; the most famous, Naumkeag, is in western Massachusetts. Use and beauty, he declared, should go hand in hand, and the garden should include "every comfort to induce people to go out of doors and live in the open. Among the most important comforts is privacy." Throughout his career as a landscape architect, Steele was always experimenting with ideas, sometimes adapting features from the great European gardens that had made a lasting impression on him during his travels.

The art of creating small gardens was brought to a new high level in the work of Loutrell Briggs, who first went to Charleston, South Carolina, in the mid-1930s and then wintered there for thirty years. Briggs was inspired to revive the beauty of those town gardens that had seen their heyday in the eighteenth and nineteenth centuries but had since suffered fires, earthquakes, hurricanes, and war damage. He made new gardens; these were small areas, often walled and irregularly shaped. Responding to these challenges, he created pleasing pictures framed by high walls and overhanging trees. He had the ability to see a garden from all angles, to make a vignette of an unpropitious corner.

Like Loutrell Briggs, Thomas Church was a master at creating small gardens. He lived and worked in San Francisco, and the tiny garden of his home, where his widow still lives, is a masterpiece. By the 1950s he was a landscape architect with a national reputation, and he continued to design gardens until his death, in 1978, adapting his concepts to the California climate and life-style. He was famous for the sensitive and clever way he included the requisite swimming pool, always difficult to disguise or hide in a small garden. His pool areas are decorative throughout the year and are integral elements, places to gather around. In larger gardens his pools fit the character of their design: in Oriental style or in free-form or circular shapes, hidden in woodland settings or open to panoramic views.

"Gardens," Church declared, "are for people," and as such they should have unity and stress function. The terrace is for outdoor living, and its scale must always be right; the entrance must be welcoming and steps must invite exploration. Thomas Church designed more than two thousand gardens and his work has a characteristic stamp, yet

The "afternoon garden" created by Fletcher Steele for Mabel Choate at Naumkeag, in western Massachusetts, was inspired by the "outdoor rooms" of Pompeian gardens, where vegetation took the place of rugs. This garden is a genuine extension of the house, with the library door leading directly onto it. Steele achieved a sense of both openness and containment by the use of a slim colonnade that frames the view without hiding it.

Among the great contributions of Thomas Church as a garden designer was his treatment of the swimming pool, an element so essential to California living. The unusual and flowing shapes he created blend into the surrounding landscape, as seen here in a private garden in Sonoma.

he prided himself on creating a green oasis to suit each individual client. As George Plumptre writes in *Garden Ornament* (Thames & Hudson, London, 1989), "Contemporary American gardens have shown a capacity to incorporate modern and abstract influences. . . . Aided by the manner in which original modern styles have been accepted in architecture, American garden designers have moved away from classical traditions more easily [than their European counterparts]."

One example of the truly individual American style is seen in the work of Wolfgang Oehme and James van Sweden. My first viewing of an Oehme and van Sweden planting was by torchlight on a cold winter evening while walking with James van Sweden through downtown Washington, D.C. The grasses looked like tall dancers clustering together, towering over mysterious, ghostly skeletons of perennials. It was the airiness of the grasses standing amid the dried flowers and leaves that was so unusual, in such strong contrast to conventional municipal borders, stripped of their tired geraniums and petunias and wearing their dreary winter look. The next morning—a bright, crisp one—I was equally struck by the natural look, a dramatic winter ground-cover collage, of James's own 55' x 16' garden.

Tall grasses, the trademark of Oehme and van Sweden, are used with shorter, low-maintenance perennials: black-eyed Susan, *Sedum* 'Autumn Joy,' purple coneflower, bergenia, nandina, ligularia, and yucca, all with leaves or seed heads that will survive well into the winter. They plan for a four-season garden that is easy to maintain—something like a cottage-garden thrown into a meadow of grasses, apparently planted at random. It is a new way of looking at space, forgetting both geometry and lawns, drawing inspiration from the surroundings, imitating nature rather than attempting to control it.

Mass plantings of *Calamagrostis acutiflora* 'Stricta', lythrum, and *Eupatorium* 'Gateway' (Joe-Pye weed) by the firm of Wolfgang Oehme and James van Sweden make a simple but dramatic setting for the swimming pool in a country garden.

In the last decade, in addition to some 250 private gardens, Oehme and van Sweden have been responsible for the planting of thirty public places. If even one in ten of the tens of thousands of people who walk by these unconventional plantings is aware of them, the message will filter through.

After the First World War, Charles Henry Gale and his brother started a landscape contracting company in Philadelphia; today, the firm works on a scale similar to that of Oehme and van Sweden. Now the remarkably successful father-and-son partnership of the next generations, Charlie and Chuck Gale, has advised and constructed many hundreds of new gardens and revitalized old ones in their individual style. They often turn to historic gardens for inspiration, to the patterned knot gardens and parterres, espaliered fruit trees, and other forms reminiscent of Louis XIV's potager at Versailles. They have been innovative in pruning and training a wide variety of shrubs, including azaleas, hollies, crab apples, rhododendrons, *Magnolia grandiflora*, *M. soulangeana*, and *Pterostyrax hispida*. Like the Renaissance architects of Italy, they view the garden as an extension of the house, reflecting the needs and personalities of the owners. Two basic tenets of their philosophy are proper preparation of the ground and the use of the best possible plants. They often supply ones of mature growth, and today, when instant results are frequently demanded, this is an approach to be valued.

A strong regional influence in the emerging American style is the garden designer James David of Austin, Texas. Here the climate in summer is difficult for gardens; in his own he has achieved a succession of lushness by using vine arbors for shade and native Texan "desert-edge" plants, as well as Mediterranean ones, to contend with the dry heat. He is helping to overcome the entrenched attitude that a summer garden is impossible in Texas, just as Ryan Gainey is doing in Georgia.

James David's semi-arid garden in central Texas is constructed of native limestone pavers and river gravel, interspersed with native plants and introduced species. In the fall it is highlighted by *Zinnia angustifolia, Heliotropium arborescens* 'Iowa', and red *Gomphrena globosa*.

Authors of garden books and regular horticulture columns have a wider audience than landscape architects, and consequently they may well have a broader influence. Henry Mitchell writes a weekly column, "Earthman," in the *Washington Post* (a collection of these columns was published as *The Essential Earthman* [1978]). He has his own garden in Washington and writes only about plants he has grown and handled himself, so you can be sure his knowledge is based on fact. He also writes about the garden structures he likes—lily pools, walks, straight brick paths, plants to screen out other people's houses. His opinions are sometimes whimsical and often unorthodox enough to make one sit up and think, remember, perhaps copy.

Like Oehme and van Sweden, the writer and photographer Ken Druse is a believer in the natural garden, working with rather than against nature, using native plants, hardy perennials, and ornamental grasses, a direction he promoted in *The Natural Garden* (1989).

Successful gardening requires humor as well as knowledge and hard work, and all are well supplied by the distinguished practicing horticulturist Fred McGourty. In his remarkable garden in northwestern Connecticut he propagates and sells unusual perennials suited to American gardens. However, he is best known for his writing. For many years he edited the excellent Brooklyn Botanic Garden series; his own book *Perennials: How to Select, Grow and Enjoy* (1985; with Pamela Harper) has been very successful, and his latest, *The Perennial Gardener*, will doubtless be equally so, as more and more people show an interest in perennial plants.

Allen Lacy, now one of America's best-known gardening writers, shares his gardening philosophy as a regular columnist in the *New York Times*. He also brought the vast correspondence of Elizabeth Lawrence of Charlotte, North Carolina, to a broad audience, publishing her "market bulletins" as *Gardening for Love* (1987). His anthology, *The American Gardener: A Sampler* (1988), is a discerning selection of garden writings from the nineteenth and twentieth centuries.

With Sir John Thouron we have come full circle: he is a modern-day settler from Scotland with a Scottish head gardener. The magnificent fifteen-acre garden he has created in the Brandywine Valley is designed to look appealing from all parts of his house. With his visitors he strolls along a planned route, passing his specialities: perennial beds, scarlet willows and heaths, a shade garden, a stream, and an alpine garden. It is a place united in spirit by the festival of flowers Sir John has brought from Britain and from the world over. He has a distinctive style of planting, using bright colors that can "take" the strong Pennsylvania sunshine. These he mixes in bold sweeps, as in the meadow garden, where he grows European field flowers, harvesting his own seeds each autumn. His planting of perennials reminds me of the traditional herbaceous borders in Scottish gardens. In Scotland they are at their best in August and September, but in Pennsylvania the peak occurs during the second week of June.

Sir John's garden is beyond the scale and scope of most present-day private gardeners, and it differs in its basic concept from most American gardens. But through his original approach he has achieved a dramatic adaptation of traditional plants in an American setting, under an American sky.

I have chosen in this introduction to give a brief survey of men who I believe have influenced gardening in America, rather than to analyze the philosophies and interests of the writers of these twenty-seven essays. It is interesting to note, however, that many of the themes I have explored recur in the pages that follow. American gardeners are still carving out new gardens from virgin soil or farmland—among them Bob Dash in Long Island, Joseph Eck and Wayne Winterrowd in Vermont, and Marshall Olbrich and the late Lester Hawkins in California. Frank Cabot, Harold Epstein, Cecil Smith, and John Fairey are travelers and plant collectors.

William Frederick has made a large garden on rolling Delaware farmland, planting in broad sweeps of color in the style of Roberto Burle Marx. He is an artist in his planting. And so is Marco Polo Stufano, curator of the gardens at Wave Hill in New York; I remember his saying, "Real gardening is picture making—the garden is your palette." William Banks's garden, with its fountain and formal boxwood, is colonial in style within its Repton-influenced landscape, while the city lots of Jimmy Graham and Ryan Gainey are spiritual descendants of the early town gardens, making a small space into a personal paradise. Both men have been inspired by English gardens. Liddon Pennock, using clipped boxwood for walls and ornaments, has adapted the fashion of garden rooms to suit present-day life-styles, reminding me of Fletcher Steele's idiom. Harland Hand has disproved the cliché that "There is nothing new in gardening" by setting plants among concrete/bedrock structures, reflecting the Sierran landscape he loves.

One thing is certain and exciting: creative gardening is becoming an everyday hobby for many more people. In recent years plant centers and specialist nurseries have proliferated, and there has been a change of attitude about using native plants in garden settings. Stimulating all of this are the increasing opportunities for amateurs, as well as professionals, to learn about everyday horticulture, garden history, and garden style. In these four centuries, American gardening has come a very long way; I leave the readers of this book to decide how it will develop in the future.

BARNSLEY HOUSE
DECEMBER 1989

A sweeping herbaceous border in the spectacular Brandywine Valley garden of Sir John Thouron is typical of his bold plantings in its scale and brilliant color.

Overleaf: Border, arbor of *Juniperus virginiana*, and greenhouse in the garden of Ryan Gainey.

THE AMERICAN
MAN'S GARDEN

William Banks

The classical portico of the house, which was built in 1828, is framed by a pair of water oaks on the terrace, with a clump of white azaleas ('Snow') in the foreground.

The doorway and fanlight of the early-nineteenth-century house frame the view of terrace, *tapis vert*, and lake.

ONLY THE EDITOR'S BENEVOLENCE can explain my inclusion in a book of expert gardeners. I do not cultivate old roses, with their subtle fragrance and brief blooming span, or exotics of any species, nor do I scour the woods and fields for the fragile wildflowers that, when transplanted to one's garden, must be nourished with a medicine dropper and admired with a magnifying glass. Like my parents before me, I strive for mass effects, and I am unscrupulous about the means of achieving them. I shock friends who are serious gardeners when I confess to buying bedding plants by the hundreds for instant color, and to treating bulbs and biennials like annuals, yanking them up the moment the blossoms fade. I plant too many flowers and shrubs too close together, and I applaud the survival of the fittest.

As a gardener, I have had the good fortune to inherit two invaluable assets. The first is a landscape garden with excellent bones, designed in the 1920s and early '30s by my father in collaboration with a professional landscape architect, the late William C. Pauley of Atlanta. The second is a small corps of gardeners, most of whom have worked at Bankshaven for many years and who take the same pride in the place that I do. The oldest, Young Turner, who is over eighty, has been here for half a century.

The principal vista, with its expanse of turf bordered by clumps of trees and shrubs and its small lake, owes an obvious debt to Capability Brown, that obsessive advocate of the picturesque; but it is even closer in spirit to Brown's great successor, Humphry Repton. While retaining Brown's picturesque features, Repton preferred to separate the park from the house with a terrace, and he reintroduced, near the house, the formal flower gardens that Brown had ruthlessly eliminated, decorated with fountains and sculptural ornaments. America's pioneer landscape architect, Andrew Jackson Downing, was a disciple of Repton, and Downing's influence on early-twentieth-century designers such as William Pauley probably accounts for the Reptonian aspects of Bankshaven. The counterpoint between my neoclassical house—which was built near Milledgeville, Georgia, in 1828 and dismantled and moved to its present site in 1970—and the early-twentieth-century landscape design inspired by Repton is, I think, wonderfully harmonious.

The south facade of the house commands a grassy rise that slopes from an oak-shaded terrace to the lake. The far shore of the lake is forested, and in the spring a multitude of dogwood (*Cornus florida*) and redbud (*Cercis canadensis*) is reflected in the still water. On the east side of the house, set at an angle to the main axis of lawn and lake—very much in the style of Repton, incidentally—is a series of formal gardens. The first, defined by a nine-foot-high boxwood hedge (*Buxus sempervirens*), features a three-tiered marble fountain with water spouting from the mouths of lions and dolphins, which

The focal point of a formal garden is a mid-nineteenth-century marble fountain. This green and white garden is framed by a boxwood hedge and, in the borders in April, by stately white tulips.

was imported from Italy in the 1840s for an Italianate villa in the hills of northern Georgia.

A few steps to the north of the fountain, through a wrought-iron arbor festooned with the white Lady Banks rose, is the most secluded of the gardens. It is hidden by hydrangea trees (*Hydrangea paniculata* 'Grandiflora') that produce masses of giant snow-balls in August, and bordered by scarlet 'Hinodegiri' azaleas that provide brilliant color in April. This secret garden is presided over by two marble sisters, a lissome *Spring* and a rather stocky *Autumn*; like the fountain, they were sculpted in Italy in the mid–nineteenth century.

Just south of the fountain, a double flight of steps leads down to the swimming pool, which is surrounded by a clipped holly hedge (*Ilex fosteri*). The tentlike pool house, trimmed with plumes and pineapples, boasts a distant kinship to the splendid Chinese pavilion at Drottningholm. An opening in the hedge leads to the most tenebrous of the formal gardens: a maze of century-old dwarf boxwood (*Buxus sempervirens* 'Suffruticosa') shaded by dogwoods, a white flowering peach, and pink and white Japanese cherries. In the 1930s my father transplanted the boxwood from a cousin's place, and the head gardener at that time tagged and numbered the plants as they were dug, so that when they were replanted in their new setting they fitted together like the pieces of a jigsaw puzzle to replicate the original design. At the upper end of the maze the sinuous walks

A secluded garden, shaded by dogwood, features a marble statue of Spring and, in August, the massed white blossoms of *Hydrangea paniculata* 'Grandiflora'.

At the apex of a maze of century-old dwarf boxwood (*Buxus sempervirens* 'Suffruticosa'), a trellised gazebo is framed by a pair of Japanese cherries.

converge on a pentagonal trellised gazebo with ogee arches, and at the lower end, on a vast rectangular flower garden laid out in a geometric pattern and protected by a wall of old brick.

The landscape design has remained virtually the same for more than half a century, but there have been planting changes dictated by the vagaries of fashion and the vicissitudes of climate. Over the years the cringing Pfitzer juniper and the pernicious privet, a breeding ground for whitefly, have been judiciously supplanted, and the blatant cannas were weeded out of the flower borders years ago.

More recently I have had to find substitutes for the victims of record-breaking cold (8° below zero in January 1985!) and unprecedented drought. Along a woodland path I have replaced all the beautiful *Camellia japonica*—a joy since my childhood—with cold-resistant mountain laurel (*Kalmia latifolia*), and around the stumps of the great photinias that once screened the several gardens, I have planted sturdy American holly (*Ilex opaca*) and graceful cherry laurel (*Laurocerasus caroliniana*). In a few years, if the weather is benign, the gardens will once again be hidden from each other.

Some of the changes in the flower gardens are the result of my increasing preference for simple effects and my fondness for white. In the borders of the fountain garden, for

The walled flower garden in May is a jigsaw in pink and white. There are peonies in the middle beds, and the Floribunda roses (pink 'Betty Prior' and rose-colored 'Improved Lafayette') are at the height of bloom. The armillary sphere at the bottom of the garden is seen again below, in a view from the opposite direction that shows its position on an axis with the gazebo in the boxwood garden. It is surrounded by fibrous begonias, which blend with the lavender and pink foxgloves, the blue pansies, and the white daisies in the border.

One of the tribe of peacocks at Bankshaven preens on the branch of an oak tree on the terrace.

In early April the borders of the walled garden are brilliant with red and yellow tulips ('Balalaika' and 'Golden Age'), pink sweet William, and blue pansies. The blossoms of a dozen dogwood trees overhang the ivy-covered walls.

example, I have replaced the multicolored tulips of past years with white varieties (now the lily-petaled 'White Triumphator'), and in summer I plant white impatiens. The green and white combination is refreshing on hot days, and for the impatiens I have a historical precedent: Roland Green, in *A Treatise on the Cultivation of Ornamental Flowers*, published in Boston in 1828—the year my house was built—and said to be the first American book to concern itself wholly with flowers, asserts that impatiens is "a very fine annual plant, with great abundance of showy flowers."

The large walled flower garden is much as it was in my mother's time: in five of the beds there are Floribunda roses (pink 'Betty Prior' and rose-colored 'Improved Lafayette'); five beds still have the peonies she planted in the 1940s; and the three beds at the bottom of the garden are filled annually with white and pink fibrous begonias. The long borders, which change dramatically from season to season, also remain essentially the way she planned them, with drifts of harmonizing colors in rhythmic repetition. There are yellow and red tulips and blue pansies and Dutch iris in the early spring; sweet William and daisies in May; daylilies (*Hemerocallis* 'Hyperion'), pink and white zinnias, marigolds, and cleome in the summer; and chrysanthemums in the fall.

The basic scheme has depended largely on bulbs and annuals, but since the early 1970s I have been gradually inserting more and more perennials. First I introduced *Phlox paniculata* 'White Admiral', then pink and white astilbe, stokesia, and *Sedum spectabile*; and in the past few years I have experimented with coreopsis, monarda, bearded iris, veronica, and physostegia. The coreopsis is a lifesaver in late May, when the spring garden is fading and the summer blooms have not yet appeared, and last summer, for the first time, the monarda ('Croftway Pink') really distinguished itself. This garden is a parade of blossom from late February through November.

Of course, like most gardeners, I experience frequent disappointments, and at those times the resident fowl at Bankshaven provide a lively distraction. Dazzling peacocks shriek and preen on terrace and lawn, and on the lake there are comical ducks and stately, cruel swans that sometimes indulge their oedipal impulse to destroy their fathers and seduce their mothers.

I mentioned disappointments. I should have said *disasters*! On the days when everything goes wrong—wild dogs break up a peahen's nest, a tulip bed that was supposed to be yellow turns out to be red, a clump of phlox inexplicably withers—on those days I regard Georgia's lengthy gardening season not as a boon but as a prolongation of misery. In addition to the malignant weather conditions of the past few years, we have had to cope with such familiar pests as aphid, whitefly, and red spider mite, as well as with newcomers such as gypsy moth and Japanese beetle; and of course botrytis, black spot, and mildew endureth forever. One wonders whether an extensive garden is worth the labor, time, and emotional commitment it demands.

And then, inevitably, there comes a morning when the spring sun glitters on the lake and stripes the lawn with shadows, when the elusive scent of boxwood mingles with the fragrance of pale, shaggy peonies, when hosts of early daisies cluster about the spires of foxgloves and hundreds of rosebuds flutter in the breeze. One savors the euphoric moment, and then grabs a trowel and attacks the chickweed that is threatening to strangle the begonias.

I T WAS WITH GREAT HESITANCY that I accepted the invitation to join the other gentlemen represented in this book. For the past twenty-two years, rather than making my own private garden, I have been involved in developing plantings on twenty-eight acres of land owned since 1960 by the people of the City of New York. Formerly the private estate of the Perkins-Freeman family, Wave Hill is now a public institution open 363 days a year. I cannot deny, however, that I have always felt that the place could perhaps best achieve its horticultural niche if it consciously attempted to maintain its former domestic ambience and purposefully avoided institutional aesthetics. What has emerged, I am often told, is a garden that, at least in part, reflects individual taste and personality.

A second reason for my initial reluctance was that in no way have I been solely responsible for the creation of the garden as it is today; over the years the entire horticultural staff has had significant input. But there was one person — sadly now gone — who was my collaborator for some twenty years. John H. Nally, a young man from the Midwest with a master's degree in printmaking and no formal horticultural training, was sent up to Wave Hill by Elizabeth C. Hall, that great lady of American horticulture. John joined our staff as a weekend admissions person and part-time gardener. He had a keen interest in plants and gardens — his art, in fact, had been primarily concerned with them — and he soon became a topflight plantsman, gardener, and colleague. I too was at the beginning of my career, and virtually a novice; together we plodded on and managed to learn a thing or two. John eventually became Wave Hill's first Curator of the Gardens. In April 1988 he died. He was instrumental in all I am going to describe in this essay, and without his creative energy and input I am not sure what direction the development of our garden philosophy and style might have taken. His spirit and love of plants, gardens, and all things beautiful will remain with me, my staff, and the garden to guide us each day in our horticultural and aesthetic decisions.

Looking back across the years, I find it difficult to remember where the ideas came from initially or why the designs and plantings took the course they did. Roughly half of Wave Hill's twenty-eight acres is woodland, the rest being devoted to gardens and lawns. Within this cultivated area there are two smaller gardens, which I would like to focus on, as they are the most personal and perhaps the most interesting from a plantsman's point of view. They are "the wild garden" and "the flower garden."

The wild garden is located on the highest land at Wave Hill. Some of the inspiration for its development came from the gardens at Fort Tryon Park, about three miles south of us, near the Cloisters Museum; like Wave Hill, they occupy a piece of land at the

The flower garden early on a May morning, with the sun highlighting the Hudson River and the Palisades of New Jersey beyond. In the lower left-hand corner *Crambe cordifolia* is in full bloom.

The hard, smooth, buff-toned surface of a strawberry jar is played against a profusion of columbine and the dwarf *Syringa patula* 'Miss Kim'.

Siberian iris and *Phlox pilosa ozarkana* clothe the bones of the wild garden with fleeting color. Two silver-frosted spires of *Verbascum bombyciferum* echo the strong perpendicular shapes of the chamaecyparis.

crest of a ridge overlooking the Hudson River. This highest point is capped by a rustic gazebo reached by a casual network of meandering paths, which we have left basically as we found them. When I arrived, in 1967, the plants remaining here were few and far between, and weeds were rampant — in fact, we eliminated great patches of bind-weed simply by covering areas with black plastic for two seasons and turning our attention elsewhere.

Until a few years ago I would have said that the major shrubs in the wild garden were inherited, but two of the largest chamaecyparis were actually grown from rooted cuttings I brought with me on my arrival. Gardens, as we all know, are living, breathing organisms; change is what they are about. The chamaecyparis are now out of scale and must soon be removed, but the clumps of shadbush and hedge maple remain from

ESTATE GARDENS

In the "wild garden" the yellow, orange, and white of helianthemum, draba, and iberis are sharpened by association with the pale blue of *Phlox divaricata*.

former days, as does the japonesque cut-leaf sumac dominating the center of the wild garden. The gazebo sits in a cloudlike mantle of yews; these had grown akimbo but many years ago were pruned tightly to become the restful architectural anchor of this garden. Some years ago we planted a *Pinus parviflora glauca* just next to the summerhouse entrance. Our thought was that its branches would eventually swoop across the gazebo roof in great arcs, and three years ago we saw this beginning to happen.

While establishing the main framework of the wild garden, we voraciously acquired and tried out plants from everywhere. We were especially drawn to species of wild plants, seed of which we ordered from the exchange lists of plant societies and botanical gardens. To us the site called for casual and quasi-natural plantings; hybrid prima donnas seemed inappropriate. What has come about through trial and error and combined gut and

aesthetic reactions is a mixed landscape of bulbs and herbaceous and woody plants arranged in a loose yet, we hope, controlled manner. We began to call it the wild garden because we saw it as a landscape "which looks as though it has occurred naturally but is made up of plants hailing from all parts of the world." Lengthy discussions have taken place about the aptness of the name—the garden is not quite what William Robinson had in mind, nor is it the native plant garden that most Americans think of when they hear those words. The name, however, remains.

One of the great joys of the wild garden and also perhaps the element that gives it its special vitality is our reliance on the "rightness" of self-sown plants. Everything from *Gentiana scabra* to *Asclepias tuberosa* and giant verbascums comes and goes with only light—though we hope artful—selective thinning. Quite a few years ago a member of the office staff brought us a bloodroot seedling she had found growing in her garden. Being a petunia-and-marigold type herself, she did not recognize its merit. We planted it beneath the shadbush, in one of the few shady patches we had at the time, and it has since seeded itself all over, with no regard for the fact that the silty, sunny areas it chooses bear no resemblance to its original and supposedly required woodland habitat.

Over the years we have found that some of our most precious seedlings appear in the paths; the gravel obviously makes a desirable seedbed. Rather than meticulously pulling them all out to assure an unobstructed way for our visitors, we leave many of them where they are. This, along with the narrowing of several paths to a space barely wide enough for one person to pass through, helps to give the gardens a noninstitutional look. Even after a busy weekend we find far less damage from careless footsteps than might be

Some fifteen years ago we introduced the first precious seedlings of purple-leaved fennel into the "wild garden." Since then it has sown itself prolifically and is here seen as a foil for *Allium giganteum*, backed by a curtain of frosty-blue *Cedrus libani atlantica* 'Glauca Pendula'.

For a few brief days in the middle of October the cut-leaved staghorn sumac (*Rhus typhina laciniata*) steals the spotlight in the wild garden. Its golden fire is heightened by the purple Mexican mealy cup sage (*Salvia leucantha*) and white pearly everlasting (*Anaphalis triplinervis*). Special effort has gone into making fall perhaps the most spectacular season at Wave Hill.

Opposite: A close-up of Wave Hill's "monocot garden" shows not only the diversity of this group of plants but also the dramatic textural and color effects that can be achieved.

imagined; in fact I think that our horticultural obstacle course causes people to slow down, perhaps even to look more closely. Purpose enough for a public garden to exist!

The area at the front of the greenhouse was formerly a rose garden with grass paths, but some five years ago we set out to remake it. We did this for several reasons. First of all, soon after we opened to the public it was apparent that hard-surfaced paths were called for. Also, a healthy American elm tree just to the south of the garden (one of the five remaining at Wave Hill) was casting more and more shade. Finally, hybrid tea roses are not the ideal plants for New York's climate, and they require an excessive amount of repetitious spraying and maintenance.

With no appropriate place to grow such things as hybrid peonies, iris, and other more "cultivated" herbaceous plants, we decided to turn this area into a flower garden. Plans were made to have the main paths put down in brick pavers, but the work was to be done on city contract, which is always a waiting game. For two seasons we put in a temporary "$16.30 garden"—a garden of annuals that we grew from seed costing that amount. I am certain we were influenced by distant memories of the annual borders at Nymans in Great Britain. It was a great hit and gave us a chance to play with the soft and undulating style of planting that we hoped to achieve eventually in our intended scheme.

The main paths finally went in, and we installed slate on the secondary paths ourselves. Over the years of waiting we had begun to acquire the plants for this garden. In a nod toward the period in which Wave Hill was originally developed by the Perkins family, we decided to use only earlier cultivars of peonies, iris, and clematis. Fortunately *Paeonia* 'Le Cygne', *Iris* 'Gracchus', and *Clematis* 'Madame André', to name just a few, are still among the most desirable to be had.

Several climbing roses remain from the original garden. At the corners of the rustic fence surrounding the area are two glorious 'Silver Moon' roses with large single white blooms, and 'Doctor Van Fleet' and a sumptuous pink-flowered climber recently identified as 'Madame Gregoire Staechelin' grow over the covered seats on either side of the garden.

It was clear from the beginning that in order to have "bones," the flower garden needed a certain amount of shrubbery. We planted *Syringa* 'Miss Kim', *Buddleia davidii* 'Nanho Blue' and *B.d.* 'Fortune', several 'Sea Foam' roses, and a few lace-cap hydrangeas. One of the beds has been developed with a red theme, anchored visually by *Gleditsia triacanthos* 'Rubylace', *Cotinus coggygria* 'Royal Purple', and a purple-leaved plum, all of them cut back each year.

As it goes into its fifth full season, the flower garden is due for a major overhaul. Some parts still lack underlying structure, and more shrubs are needed—up from the nursery will come a variegated kerria, *Hydrangea macrophylla* 'Tokyo Red', *Rhamnus frangula* 'Asplenifolia', and perhaps a boxwood or two. We are trying hard not to belabor decisions about their placement. This in fact is a policy that we try to follow throughout the garden; too often in the past we have been paralyzed, albeit temporarily, by the hope of a perfect solution. Now, with a few years of experience and accumulated intuition behind us, we hope to be freer in trying things and then simply changing them if they do not work. In terms of both the grounds and the greenhouses, ours is much too small a garden to present the world with a perfect solution: we have no extensive growing areas where we can experiment or hold plants until we are certain of their merit. Perhaps it is best that way, for it allows the public an opportunity to see the process of gardening in all the stages of its development, in its failed aesthetic experiments and its occasional glorious moments.

The May lushness of *Rosa* 'Königin von Dänemark', *Clematis* 'Ville de Lyon', *Iris* 'Fra Angelico', and *Paeonia lactiflora* 'Madame de Verneville' contrasts with the pyramidal geometry of chamaecyparis and junipers.

Opposite, top: Among the many older cultivars of iris used in the flower garden is *Iris* 'Honorabile', seen here with *Rosa* 'Mary Wallace' and a purple-leaved sand cherry, which is cut back each season.

Opposite, bottom: *Atriplex hortensis* 'Rubra', *Dahlia* 'Bishop of Llandaff', *Gleditsia triacanthos* 'Rubylace', and *Crocosmia* 'Lucifer' are just a few of the plants in the red section of the flower garden. The gleditsia, normally a tree, is cut back each season.

J. Liddon Pennock, Jr.

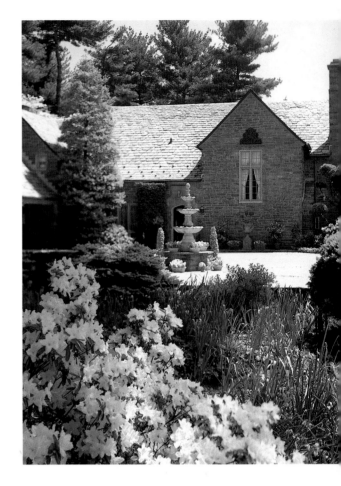

The motor-court entryway, with the stone-tiered drip fountain forming an effective centerpiece. *Ilex opaca*, to the left of the door, forms an emphatic, well-pruned green column that nicely balances the spire-shaped chimney on the right. The azalea in the foreground is 'Delaware Valley White'.

MY FOREBEARS FLED ENGLAND during the final years of the seventeenth century, following William Penn to seek homesteads in what is now known as Pennsylvania. These hardy souls emigrated because of their desire to escape the pomp and titled circumstance, to return to the simple life, with an emphasis on agriculture in all its exciting forms. Many of these early settlers either were given land grants by Penn himself or else purchased large tracts from those who were. The latter was the case, at many generations' remove, for the present owners of Meadow-brook Farm.

Our place is located north of Philadelphia, on a twenty-five-acre sliver of what a generation or so before was a real working farm, with all of the accouterments, including cattle, horses, and farm crops. Hence the residual name—Meadowbrook Farm.

After several years spent at the Agricultural College of Cornell University, I married at the age of twenty-two, and building a proper home became a necessity. The house was started in 1935 and completed in 1936. It was poised on the brow of a fairly precipitous slope that at the outset seemed to present an enormous problem. The architect felt that a long, impressive driveway leading to the front of the house was paramount, and that the rear was secondary. We soon discovered that the reverse was true.

The architect designed the two level flagstone terraces off the center hall, the dining room, and the living room, on the south side of the house. It was actually the inter-relationship between the two areas that pointed out the direction in which the overall design of the future gardens would proceed. The upper terrace, off the dining room, was obviously intended for outdoor meals, and the lower terrace was to be the place where we and our guests would assemble to sit and talk before dinner. Each terrace area would reflect the role of its counterpart within the house.

Our idea was to transfer our mode of indoor living into a garden environment, or duplicate it there, but the sudden drop-off of these terraces at the outset precluded any hope of their echoing the facilities within the house. Soon the solution became startlingly evident. What we needed was a plan that would include garden rooms for the various activities that make a house a home, locations for welcoming guests, for dining, for resting, for conversation, for reading, and for contemplation. A bath is vital in the house, so why not have one outside? This idea actually points out the wisdom of having a small garden and contributes immensely to the joys of being closely involved with nature and all of its bounties.

Our next move was to study proportion and scale, since our thought was that the garden must never overwhelm the building but always complement it.

Protected by overhanging trees, the black-framed gazebo blends into the gray-green scheme of planting and statuary. The green marbleized inserts reflect the variegated aucuba beneath. Beside these, a pair of *Hedera canariensis* trained on wire frames reach up toward the Boston fern baskets (*Nephrolepis exaltata* 'Aurea'), which retain their golden color through exposure to strong sun in the mornings only.

The pink ivy geranium 'Roi des Balcons' cascades from a tall marble urn, in pleasant contrast to the blue *Plumbago auriculata* tumbling between two wood and cast-iron chairs on the terrace of a dipping pool.

Two Sargent weeping hemlocks have been bonsaied to keep them at the proper height, below the wings of the eighteenth-century lead eagle, and *Buxus suffruticosa* 'Sempervirens' has been clipped to maintain its height at fifteen inches for over fifty years. The four beds are massed with *Salvia farinacea* and pink New Guinea hybrid impatiens.

All of our plans had to be minimal in concept. In the thirties the economy of our country was at its lowest ebb, so we had to be totally aware of emphasizing low maintenance costs. Both of our lives were busy, with my wife deeply involved in volunteer duties, and me working ten days a week in a center-city florist establishment started by my grandfather and given to me by my father. At Meadowbrook our sole helper was an aged Polish gardener, who was fortunately both strong and eager.

Many people have asked me whether in the beginning I made or conceived an entire overall concept. Frankly, I did not. Our first major project was to create a flat space off the existing terrace to play the part of the central hall in the house, with arms leading away from the building. We needed to create a series of small level areas out of the original precipitous hillside, and this meant undertaking a major grading job on three levels.

First we installed a wall thirty feet or so away from the south side of the terraces, then filled it with soil to bring the area up even with the base of the house, thus creating a space for our first flat garden room. The stone wall matched the house, with heavy flagstone copings repeating the surface of the terrace. It then became axiomatic that this type of building material be repeated in all of the basic masonry work that was to be added later.

Stairs were built from this new level down to the next. When the upper level was finished it featured a low boxwood hedge in the form of a circle. An impressive eighteenth-century lead eagle with a six-foot wingspan was placed on the low wall directly opposite the middle of the living-room terrace; a lead cistern, housing a small jet of water, was set against the wall below it. This focal point was the inspiration for the name of the first garden—the Eagle Garden.

ESTATE GARDENS

The circular center beds surrounding the fountain pool are defined by Belgian blocks, as are the four outer beds. Color comes from the "cocktail mix" of fibrous-rooted begonias. The miniature green hedge behind the begonias (bottom right) is stephanandra. The gazebo, which is English, probably nineteenth-century, has limestone pillars and cornice and a restored wrought-iron dome.

A black cast-iron fence led from the corner of the dining terrace out to the new retaining wall, making a wide, square space edged with boxwood in a semicircle. Each bed is planted with masses of spring, summer, and fall flowers according to the season. The opening of the iron fence on the east was located exactly opposite the entrance steps to the lower, west garden. This completed the beginning of the main east-west axis of the future gardens.

Twelve steps, their risers clad in ivy, provided easy access from the Eagle Garden to the lower level, where a small circular pool formed the centerpiece. The even spacing of the paths was emphasized by their edging of Belgian block. Today the content of this lower garden, but not its structure, has been altered to obtain a landscape with an Italianate feeling, where tall, slim juniper spires back figures of the Four Seasons.

Originally a semicircular *Ilex opaca* hedge provided the necessary end feature opposite the steps. Several years later we removed this hedge and installed another set of flagstone

steps of the same size and style as those to the east. These steps lead down to the large rectangular plateau, again made by removing soil from one side of the slope and using it to build up the other side. The entire area is surrounded by a low stone wall.

We then installed a small swimming pool, its outline following the same lines as the outer walls. At the far west end of the pool a bathhouse–dressing room provided an emphatic terminal feature.

The next project was to continue the progress to the east of the Eagle Garden. The path, eight feet wide and bordered by low brick walls, proceeds past a planting of semihardy shrubs such as *Camellia japonica*, *Daphne odora*, photinia, crape myrtle, and *Magnolia grandiflora*, all of which thrive under the sheltered south lee of the house and in the high shade provided by the limbed-up white pine trees, which have grown to spectacular size during the intervening years. In this special place we located a tiny heated pool equipped with a Jacuzzi and a water-spouting frog at the far end.

Then came the herb and lettuce garden, conveniently placed next to the kitchen. This garden was patterned with severely shaped squares and rectangles, all with brick or flagstone edging; the paths were made entirely of Brazilian red shale. The small, easily workable beds are filled with an interesting mix of annual and perennial herbs and areas of massed lettuce.

The final terminus for the east end of the garden's main axis is a lattice gazebo with a unique lead roof. It is set off by masses of billowy boxwood and assorted broadleaf evergreens and is entered through a semicircular brick wall, in the opening of which stands a wrought-iron gate with a pair of bronze cats guarding the entryway. Since the flagstones in the dining terrace have been replaced with old brick and since brick is featured throughout the premises as edging, we felt authorized to continue its use in this wall and in the path next to the herb garden leading to it.

Container-grown plants abound in all of the gardens at Meadowbrook Farm. Since walls occur throughout, all of them broken by entryways, pairs of planters are a real requirement everywhere. Pot plants give us the opportunity to introduce into the gardens in spring, summer, and fall many tender specimens that are compelled to languish in the cool greenhouse during the cold winter months.

Somehow or other we have attained the questionable status of being overgazeboed. Since Meadowbrook Farm has long been an exhibitor, on a noncompetitive basis, in the peerless Philadelphia Flower Show, we have always incorporated some of these gazebos in the landscape. We feel that the plethora of structures gives a garden personality, instilling a feeling of shape, style, and permanence.

Those who visit the gardens seem to be charmed by the realization that despite all of the complexity and beauty of the place, it was created entirely by the owner from start to finish, transformed from fields and a treeless hillside into a mature and highly developed landscape that belies the fact that it has existed for a mere half century.

The turf path is edged with brick so that the perennials can spill out naturally without invading the grass. The upright and cross members of the structure at the end of the path are of solid wood trimmed with plastic moldings and topped with pineapple finials made of cement, all antiqued to give a gray, weathered appearance.

The allée effect is attained by the use of low pyramidal hedges: in the foreground, *Chamaecyparis obtusa* 'Nana', and on the upper level, *Euonymus japonicus* 'Microphyllus'. Four *Hedera helix* 'Glacier', trained in cones, accentuate the two brick steps. On the right, standard *Poncirus trifoliata* are pruned into circular shapes.

W E BEGAN THE GARDEN at Stonecrop in 1959, next to a weekend house sited on a hilltop so as to enjoy the sweeping views of the Hudson Highlands. Successively larger fenced enclosures were built to protect the plantings from marauding herds of deer, until today some twenty acres are enclosed, with about half the area intensively cultivated. Initially an alpine nursery with some vegetable and perennial beds, Stonecrop now consists of a series of gardens stretching toward the seclusion of a woodland and respite from the north winds that ensure Zone 5 conditions at its 1,100-foot elevation. Unreliable and variable snow and ice cover in winter and the debilitating heat and humidity of the muggs of August in the Hudson River valley add to the challenges of creating and maintaining a garden here.

Over the years, we have built windbreaks and protective walls, introduced water features (which invariably leak), moved giant rocks, and exposed massive rock ledges. The soil was so stony that it not only gave the place its name but had to be dug two feet deep and then trucked away and replaced with new soil to render the garden cultivable.

Despite the obstacles, we have made progress. The early overcrowding of trees and shrubs and the lack of a rational structure have gradually been corrected; the gardens now have an architectural framework and relate sensibly to the house and stable. Our enthusiasm for alpine plants, which originally manifested itself in a "collector's zoo," is now expressed in a series of ordered, geometric raised stone beds and a rock-cliff planting by a new lake, where the plants have an affinity with their setting.

There is at least one season when each part of the garden comes into its own. The alpines embellish their raised beds from late April through May, and the woodland garden is full of interest in June. Midsummer sees an apotheosis of the enclosed English flower garden, followed by the tawny exuberance of the grass garden, which shows to best advantage against an autumnal woodland backdrop.

Not everything grows, of course. Ericaceous plants dislike the exposure as well as the quality of the well water, despite the fact that the woodland is thick with native stands of mountain laurel. Plants suited to more northerly climes, such as Asiatic primulas and meconopsis, do even worse here. But a *Gunnera manicata* is well into its fifth summer, with leaves five feet in diameter (thanks to careful protection in winter), and

Flower borders stretch from the house toward the enclosed flower garden and the stable yard. Dark-purple clumps of perilla contrast with the light gray of *Helichrysum petiolatum* and the pale yellow of *Anthemis* 'E. C. Buxton'. *Allium sphaerocephalum* is highlighted against *Achillea* 'Salmon Beauty', with *Rosa* 'Bonica' in the background.

A corner of the woodland garden in spring, filled with rhododendrons, primulas, and ferns, with the duck pond in the distance.

the exotic annuals and half-hardy plants that supplement the perennials in the flower borders thrive on the summer heat and humidity.

The garden at Stonecrop reflects the vision of all those who have worked on it. The raised stone beds were the result of a persistent dream, given form in the late 1970s, of growing alpines in a geometric and formal framework near a building and escaping the difficulties of attaining a naturalistic effect. The rock work was executed by Cono Reale, a Sicilian master mason and landscape contractor of genius, who with an unerring eye gathered the large slabs of rock ledge from the surrounding woodland and placed them to build the stream garden, the lake, and other features. Franklin Faust, a professor of art, turned our rough sketches and ideas for garden seats and structures into decorative and functional features.

In recent years the borders and the enclosed flower garden, as well as their architectural framework, have been greatly improved under the guidance of Caroline Burgess, late of the Royal Botanic Gardens at Kew. Caroline has renovated the plantings completely in a program that is gradually extending to other parts of the garden; she is in charge of a full-time staff of three and at least two volunteers one day a week.

Stonecrop has grown from its amateur beginnings to a respectable size and to a degree of horticultural sophistication never dreamed of at the outset. The alpines that survive the humid summers in the alpine house and the alpine areas are still there, but they no longer dominate the scene. The borders and the flower garden, which used to be limited to perennials blooming in June and September–October, now peak between July 15 and Labor Day and are of constant interest from April until December. They are filled with unfamiliar plants, many of them tender, that deserve to be more widely used in American gardens, if one could only remember their names! (Two small plastic greenhouses overwinter anything that is not hardy, providing cuttings all winter long.)

The walls and trellises are clothed with every conceivable vine and espaliered shrub, and the flower garden now has every color of the rainbow, in one instance graded from bed to bed and in another displayed in a color wheel under and around a pleached allée

of lindens. A garden room with paneled walls and Chinese windows houses a collection of pots and planted tubs filled with exotica. A woodland garden is maturing nicely.

The garden now has a larger purpose, a justification for all the time and effort poured into it over the past thirty years: it is to become public. Our goal is to end up with the widest range of plants that can be grown on the site, so that the visitor will be exposed to what can be done in a garden in these parts if one is willing to make the effort. The plants seen in the garden will be for sale on the premises, as is the case in many English gardens.

Thus Stonecrop has evolved. Our hope is that in the future it will serve as an inspiration to those who chance upon it. Given the collection of plants and the variety of the plantings and settings, we are thinking of establishing a school of practical horticulture, something that no longer exists in the Northeast. In effect, Caroline Burgess is currently running such an enterprise for her staff, imparting the benefits of the wisdom and disciplines of Kew to those who care to learn. In time it would, it

In autumn, grasses in variety provide a display of textural contrasts in the grass garden. At left, the tall plumes of *Miscanthus sinensis* 'Silberfeder', with slender *Molinia caerulea arundinacea* 'Windspiel' behind; at center, thick, wheat-colored *Calamagrostis acutiflora* 'Stricta'; to the right, *Panicum virgatum* 'Rotstrahlbusch' with flashes of red; and closer to the foreground, bright-green *Helictorichon sempervirens*.

A diagonal path leads to the toolhouse in the enclosed flower garden. Decorative pyramidal trellises provide a home for climbers and add vertical accents to the beds. *Filipendula ulmaria* 'Flore Pleno' and *Papaver rhoeas* 'Cedric Morris' border the path in late June.

Opposite: Against the setting of a Chinese window, the yellow portion of the rainbow in the enclosed flower garden includes *Achillea* 'Moonshine', *Anthemis* 'Pale Moon', *Lilium* 'French Vanilla', and *Isatis tinctoria* (woad). Evening primrose and snakeroot serve as a background.

Right: A cat's cradle of pleached linden forms an X centered on an arbor of dwarf apples. *Gertrude Jekyll*, a straw figure holding sway over the color display above, is seen here from the rear (not her most flattering aspect) in an austere winter scene.

The view from the top of the rock ledge over the lake to the west. Three waterfalls tumble through a series of pools along the rock ledge, the crevices of which are filled with alpines.

Right: A pool in the stream garden at the top of the rock ledge is bordered with Siberian iris and a *Malus* 'Red Jade'. The glimpse of the lake in the distance is bracketed by a *Sophora japonica* 'Pendula' on the right, with a *Styrax japonicus* and *Betula papyrifera* on the left.

seems, be natural to expand these activities to include others who might wish to have such intensive training.

As the Stonecrop garden takes on a life of its own, special moments occur: wild ducks sometimes choose to make the duck pond their home for an interval, or a flock of bluebirds will appropriate the trees bordering the rock ledge, brightening the waterfalls and enlivening the tranquil vista that leads over the small lake to the Hudson Highlands to the west. But then gardening *is* a labor of love, and there is nothing more satisfying than the materialization of one's vision as the years of effort and disorder finally yield to the sought-for effect and one discovers unexpected vistas and pleasures in the result. It is conceivable that the leaks in the new lake will be overcome once and for all— and, of course, next year the plantings will be better!

Thirty years on, as I walk around the different gardens in the gloaming, I cannot deny that I feel a sense of exultation, rather akin to the full-throated enthusiasm of the bullfrogs in the duck pond as they gloat over the immense gunnera that looms at the water's edge.

      ESTATE GARDENS

WHEN WE FIRST came to this Vermont hillside, thirteen years ago, we thought to make a garden very different from the one we have created. We had lived many years in Boston, and the largely eighteenth-century design of that city and its surrounding towns had shaped our sense of what a garden should be. Boxwood hedges, brick paving, and above all a rectangularity and formality of design were what we imagined when we looked over our newly acquired and as yet uncleared patch of New England forest. It does not seem to have occurred to us that such gardens were perhaps better suited to the urban surround and flat coastal plain in which they had developed. How hard (and in the end, luckily, with what little success) the patient bulldozer operator struggled to carve out the flat ground our vision required!

The process of building is peculiarly disheartening. The rawness and disorder, the press of tasks, the disparity between the muddy woodland clearing and the garden that already flourished in our minds—all of that wore us out, and we fled to California. That summer, three thousand miles and six climate zones removed from Vermont, we saw our garden as it might really be. We were not yet, of course, gardeners. We knew a little, still too little to know how little. And we knew we would be gardeners.

An hour and a half north of San Francisco, in the heavily wooded hills of the coastal range in Sonoma County, Lester Hawkins and Marshall Olbrich had begun much as we had, twenty years before us. Western Hills was then, and is still more now, one of America's most Edenlike gardens. Blessed with a benign climate, it encompasses a range of plants far vaster than we could ever attempt in our frigid Zone 4. There we saw for the first time the grevillias, phormiums, ceanothus, and leptospermums that still enchant us and that, all of them, we are forbidden.

It was not plants (sadly) that we could take away from Western Hills, but in the end a far more valuable acquisition—the knowledge of *how* to plant. For all the dissimilarity in climate between Lester and Marshall's Mediterranean hillside and our moist, cold Appalachian ridge, the shape of the land is strikingly similar. Both gardens were cut out from the forest on rolling and sometimes steep terrain. But whereas we had thought to challenge our earth with heavy equipment and retaining walls, Lester and Marshall had acknowledged theirs as the great gift it was. What was possible in California, we suddenly saw, could also be possible in Vermont—a garden of many and varied habitats, of little worlds, of dry slope and boggy hollow, windswept field and sheltered glade. We realized

Primula japonica has seeded itself happily by a boulder along the stream—so content is this plant in our cool summers that it has become almost a weed. The fine light lettuce-green foliage remains in good condition here all summer long, providing excellent ground cover.

A view up the rose path, with the peony 'Sarah Bernhardt' on the left, followed by the excellent old-fashioned shrub rose 'Henri Martin'. On the right at the far end is one of the new Canadian Explorer roses, 'Martin Frobisher', which has the virtue of blooming all summer.

Robinia pseudo-acacia 'Frisia' spent its first winter in Vermont in the greenhouse. Now it stands at eighteen feet, dominating the back garden with a shimmering curtain of many yellows, from lime to canary. Conifers—*Thuja occidentalis* 'Holmstrup' in the front and *Taxus* x *media* 'Hicksii' behind—provide a useful contrast of dark green.

A view across the lower end of the perennial garden, looking over the enclosing yew hedge to the house and the woodland garden beyond. Here *Artemisia ludoviciana* makes an indispensable rhythm and provides a cool foil for brightly colored flowers. The silver shrub peeping over the hedge is a pollarded specimen of *Salix alba sericea*.

with a start that we had been saved, just barely, from destroying the chief beauty our garden could have. We resolved to follow, even to obey with respect, the shape of the land. Happy the beginning gardener who is given so fine and so timely a lesson.

We have learned much else from Lester and Marshall over the last dozen years. Lester is now dead, but Marshall continues to be our best garden mentor, and since our first visit we have not let a winter pass without a trip to Western Hills. We have come to share their great passion for plants, and particularly for woody plants.

One of the peculiarities of the California redwood forest, as of the Vermont hardwood forests of maple, beech, and birch, is the almost complete absence of an understory. Straight trunks rise up from the herbaceous carpet without any intermediate woody flora. Part of the delight of working our garden has been the development of a rich, natural-seeming understory. We have taught ourselves to garden in the air, filling the space between our herbaceous plants and the tops of our trees with a rustling, many-tiered garden of contrasting shapes, forms, and colors. Now we are almost as unsettled by a patch of bareness between the greater trunks as many gardeners would be by a patch of bare earth. The best of all of the small trees and shrubs of the understory is a treasured specimen of *Robinia pseudo-acacia* 'Frisia', given us by Marshall when it first appeared in this country. It spent its first winter in Vermont in the greenhouse, and when it produced its first clear butter-yellow leaves in spring they were as beautiful as any flower, and we showed off its first efforts for us in a three-inch clay pot on our coffee table.

Although we think of our garden as possessing a natural form, it is not entirely without formal features. Just to the south of the house, visible from the kitchen windows, we have allowed ourselves a small terrace hedged with boxwood and somewhat softened by the many small treasures planted in the crevices of the stones. This is the first spot in the garden to thaw in the spring, and when all the rest lies still under snow and the detritus of winter, the little terrace is ordered and blooming.

The terraced perennial garden, looking from the house toward the pastureland beyond. In the foreground, the peony 'Mrs. Franklin D. Roosevelt' is surrounded by *Geranium* 'Johnson's Blue'. Behind is a glorious beautybush (*Kolkwitzia amabilis*), and the old-fashioned clove pink, *Dianthus caryophyllus*, in a double-pink form collected at the local cemetery, spills over the low wall.

The other formal space, just beyond the terrace and separated from the garden by a high yew hedge, is an enclosed herbaceous border that has a deliberate formality, much like a drawing room. The land slopes here, as everywhere, but we have carved out three level lawns, each supported by drywalling of aged limestone. The borders that surround these lawns on every side are fourteen feet deep and planted to all the exuberant perennials that we enjoy but need to see apart from the trees, shrubs, and natural paths that are the heart of the garden. Flowers are everywhere here, but they are always subordinate to other interests of leaf or shape or textural contrast. In the perennial garden the emphasis is on flower, and all manner of ill breeding in leaf and laxness in habit is excused if the bloom is fine enough.

For the rest, the garden meanders over the hillside, through the woods, and along the stream that lies at its core. That stream was in full sparkling flood the April day we bought the land, and it did more to influence our decision to commit ourselves for life to these acres even than the mature maples and beeches that clustered along its banks and towered above it. When we began to plant, however, we started perforce at our back door. The stream seemed very far off, and we wondered when the garden would ever embrace it. But for some years now it has, and it is the one place we both visit every day. (How could we ever have supposed we would possess a garden so large that any part of it could be *unvisited* on any given day?) Though very much a part of the garden now, the stream

A view of the stream garden. The giant umbrella-leaved plant to the right is the California native *Darmera peltata*, which is surprisingly happy in Vermont.
A dusting of self-seeded pink *Primula japonica* shows farther down the stream.

speaks still of wildness and remove, and its music drowns out even the insistent sound of the telephone.

Stone walks and stepping-stone paths knit the whole of the garden together. There is a rich supply of glacial granite everywhere in these hills, coming out of the earth sometimes in fine flat plates and serving as admirable paving material, far more durable and far more in keeping with the spirit of the place than brick could ever be. Luckily, our ground grows stones, each winter's freeze thrusting up yet another layer to the surface, so we do not think we will run out.

The passions of thirteen years are everywhere apparent. We know great gardeners who specialize exclusively in alpines, in roses, in hostas, iris, or daylilies. We grow, quite simply, everything we can get our hands on, our greed for plants—for *any* plant—knowing no bounds. Antique roses form a broad double border near the house, Asiatic primulas fill the bog, hostas in embarrassing variety appear everywhere, troughs of alpines sit at the doors. But two aspects of our gardening have interested us particularly.

It is really quite cold in Vermont, and the growing season is brief. Plants that bloom early and late are prized here beyond all others, giving us the illusion that winter does not really last half the year. So we grow what braves the winter in early spring—many salix species, hamamelis, *Viburnum* x *bodnantense, Corylopsis pauciflora, Daphne mezereum* 'Alba'—and plants that will save themselves for the last warm days of autumn—*Heptacodium jasminoides, Hamamelis virginiana, Clematis maximowicziana (C. terniflora).* And everything that carries fruit or seed in winter is especially valued. Among the best are the vines *Schisandra chinensis, Ampelopsis brevipedunculata,* and *Clematis tangutica,* and the shrubs *Ilex verticillata, Rosa moyesii,* and *R. rugosa.* Near the house and the chief access paths we grow plants with interestingly colored winter stems. Among our favorites are *Rubus lasiostylus* 'Hubeiensis', the best of the "whitewashed" brambles, and *Salix acutifolia* x *caprea,* which covers its rich grape-colored twigs with a dense, powdery bloom of white.

Our other passion—really just a version of the first—is to test the received wisdom about what can and cannot withstand the rigors of our frigid climate. Not every test has brought success; for us, many plants lie just fractionally outside the realm of the possible. We have, over the years, failed with *Cornus floridus, Oxydendrum arboreum, Pinus parviflora*—the list would fill the page. But we have not lost, for example, *Stewartia koreana,* which reaches now near fifteen feet, nor *Acer griseum,* the paperbark maple, both of which the best authorities assured us would perish here. And just lately we have begun to collect bamboo, twenty species of which have endured five or more winters, the last without snow cover and with weeks at subzero temperatures.

Here in Vermont on this last day of August, fall is decidedly near. The air is cool and color already shows on the hillsides. This is for many a melancholy time, with its promise of winter and the awareness of the brief summer past. But in the garden we can look forward to the first emerging colchicum and *Cyclamen hederifolium* and all the many autumn crocus—*speciosus, zonatus, sativus, serotinus salzmannii.* Those that flower now put us in mind of spring before autumn is over. And we can pretend.

JOE ECK

Many varieties of heather (*Calluna vulgaris*) bloom along the driveway in the late summer. They are interplanted with procumbent junipers and with heath for early spring bloom.

Marshall Olbrich

WESTERN HILLS

OCCIDENTAL, CALIFORNIA

THE GARDEN AT WESTERN HILLS lies sixty miles north of San Francisco, a mile up the hill from the village of Occidental, and about six miles east of the Pacific Ocean. It is surrounded mostly by second-growth but still impressive redwood, Douglas fir, and madrone forest, interspersed with open areas planted formerly to apples but now to wine grapes or monumental suburban homes. In 1959 we —my partner, Lester Hawkins, and I—purchased three acres of fallow pastureland, a sort of bent rectangle sloping gently to the east but with a decided rise at its western boundary.

This pocket of California has an excessive amount of rainfall—some sixty inches on average—in the winter months, followed by six months of drought or derisory sprinkles. The temperature ranges from 80° to 90° in the summer down to 26° or less on some winter nights. This allows us to grow a very wide range of temperate and subtropical plants. Unfortunately, there are occasional periods of sharp frost that can cause severe damage to our more daring plantings.

Traditionally gardens are compared to paintings and analyzed in similar terms, with much attention paid to the way the colors, shapes, and masses add up to create a painting or landscape. Because of its somewhat accidental history, however, and the wide range of plants grown in it, our garden seems to me more like a rather disorganized novel or drama in which characters come and go, with the good pining away and the wicked sometimes flourishing. Moreover, I myself often forget the plot and have to be reminded by old friends, old camera slides, or such "archaeological finds" as a moldering stump in a clump of alstroemerias. Was it a paulownia? Was it a pine? No, it was a eucalyptus that, after the fashion of eucalyptus, was preparing to fall over a bowkeria shrub and had to be extracted.

It seems tidy to divide my brief account into three decades, starting with the early 1960s. During the first year or two we built two rustic houses and a barn and passed through the obligatory "organic homestead" phase, complete with a fruit orchard and a vegetable garden properly mulched, which produced such delicacies as *petit pois* that we did not have time to pick. There was the endless task of ditching the waterlogged parts of the land to allow for planting; a reasonable-sized pond was excavated (this time with a bulldozer) and the subsoil piled up to relieve the general flatness of the lower area. We planted many temperate trees and many Australian, Chilean, and South African seedlings.

Humea elegans (now *Calomeria amaranthoides*), a biennial from moist places in southeastern Australia, blooms with clouds of small, coppery, musk-fragrant flowers. Seed must be saved and sown, with fingers crossed that some may be viable.

The pond, once open and the home of Koi carp, waterlilies, and great blue herons, is now encroached upon by three spreading plants: myriophyllum, pontederia, and *Iris pseudacorus*. The narrow conifers are Serbian spruce (*Picea omorika*); to the left of them, *Leptospermum laevigatum* is in bloom.

The more tender plants were concentrated near the house, at the west (and higher) end of the land, where, we assumed, frost drainage would make for warmer conditions.

With innocence and bravado we decided to have our own arboretum on less than three acres. The inevitable result has been crowding and poor presentation of potentially striking specimens. To take a single example, our weeping sequoia (*Sequoiadendron giganteum* 'Pendulum') has behaved superbly, corkscrewing its way into the sky, providing a yearly period of suspense as to whether the leader will continue climbing or fall over and head for earth. Unfortunately, it was planted not in isolation but among other conifers and maples, so its skirts and full effect are concealed from eye and camera.

To move on with my chronicle, the 1970s were years of drought and apprehension of drought in California. Lester, who by now was designing settings for apartment complexes and condominiums, found that his plans called for more and more plants that could survive restricted water use, and our own garden, still inadequately watered by a sidehill well, had the same needs.

The garden suffered its worst disaster in December 1972. There was a week of freakish cold, when the temperature never rose above 20° and several nights went down to 14°. Pumps, sprinkler risers, and piping burst, and we lost a good third of the garden.

The disastrous frost was particularly hard on the more tender plants surrounding the house, with the result that conspicuous areas were left almost bare. These we quickly populated with drought-resistant plants: California natives including ceanothus, arctostaphylos, artemisia, and baccharis; Mediterraneans such as rock roses (cistus, halimium, and x halimiocistus) and brooms (among them the trees *Genista monosperma*, *G. aethnensis*, and *G. tenera*); and Mediterranean perennials such as rosemary, lavenders, origanums, verbascums, artemisias, and, a special favorite, phlomis species in both yellow and lavender. We also started to replant the hardier Australians and South Africans.

The following decade began with a major success: in 1980 we dug a deep vertical well, which miraculously gave us sufficient water for all of our needs. This had two unforeseen consequences. First, the sediment in the water made drip irrigation impossible, and the sprinklers rained indiscriminately on water lovers and on plants that could not tolerate water in the summer months, of which we by now had many. There were a number of fatalities, including a handsome desert shrub, *Chilopsis linearis*.

Second, our trees, which with insufficient water had been slow-growing if not static, began to grow and produced more and more *shade*. This is still a major problem, though by removing some large Mexican pines and a fir we have recovered some sunny areas. Some plants are unexpectedly shade-tolerant, but not cistus, nor most of the brooms, nor many of the lovely Mediterranean herb-type plants. What we need increasingly is ground cover and perennials that will grow in shade and tolerate the root competition of established trees. I wish I could expand on this, a favorite topic, but space allows me to single out only two star performers: *Geranium macrorrhizum* in its different color forms and *Symphytum grandiflorum*, both of them tough, not overly invasive, weed-suppressing ground covers. (We now have a clump of the golden variegated *Symphytum* 'Goldsmith', a gift from Jerry Flintoff, which we hope will increase for us.)

In around 1980 Roger Warner joined our partnership. A remarkable plantsman and a demon of energy, he had a profound effect on both garden and nursery, designing and building our propagating house and display tables and creating the nursery area much as it remains today. In this account, however, I would like to associate him especially with a somewhat new element in our garden—perennials.

In 1981 Roger and I made the first of several plant-collecting trips to England. Graham Stuart Thomas's classic *Perennial Garden Plants* had appeared a few years before and we had all but memorized it, but it was tantalizing to see the actual plants in the beds at Kew (among them *Centaurea* 'Pulchra Major', *Echinops ritro ruthenicus*, *Aster* x *frikartii* 'Mönch', and *Cosmos atrosanguineus*), discuss them with that walking encyclopedia Brian Halliwell, and *then* find them all but unavailable even in specialized nurseries. It was fun to search out these scarce plants, and it added a great deal to our garden and nursery that we were able to grow and distribute them.

Roger Warner also shaped and planted an impressive double perennial border in our lower garden. Again, the problems of maintenance have proved to be too much for our resources, and though today it is still a rather handsome mélange, with (in late summer) *Artemisia lactiflora*, *Chelone lyonii*, and tall clumps of *Echinops ritro* giving a good display, the plan is to pull it apart, using the perennials with shrubs in scattered parts of the garden, where control is easier.

Lester, by this time, had more or less retired from his landscaping work and, to a

The quaking aspen (*Populus tremuloides*) does not color well but has dramatic white trunks that show up against the fox colors of the bald cypress (*Taxodium distichum*) and (at right) the evergreen New Zealand *Hoheria sexstylosa*.

The cobalt-blue- and purple-flowered South American "walking iris," *Neomarica caerulea* (the specific name may be in doubt), blooms intermittently through the warm months. The gray-blue *Campanula primuloides* self-sows all around.

degree, from the worries of the garden. He traveled a great deal and wrote a number of gardening articles. Unfortunately, having spent some months in Turkey, he returned in June 1984 with a blood infection and, after six months of declining health, died in January 1985 with many of his projects unfulfilled. Roger Warner left the partnership at about the same time to pursue his own career, so that for some while the garden lacked care.

In the last few years the garden and the nursery have necessarily been drawn closer together. Since the nursery is the major support of the garden, we pay more attention to its needs. With the increasing sophistication of gardeners in this country, we may get a call for, say, 150 *Helleborus foetidus*, and we have to take this into account in our garden plantings. We often need a dozen stock plants in the ground where, for the garden itself, two or three would do.

My own view of the garden (often close to despair) is that the plants themselves now run the show, and our rear-guard actions of weeding, removing trees and shrubs, mulching, and planting never quite seem to catch up. Yet the garden has aspects that are undeniably attractive. The foliage textures and colors of the trees are quite opulent, and the underplantings give color in a tapestry effect that people enjoy. Here let me praise "benign weeds," those garden plants that have found things to their liking and have provided color for many years. In this category belong the annual echium hybrids, alstroemerias, *Nigella damascena*, *Salvia forsskahlii*, *Campanula primuloides*, *Lychnis coronaria*, *Linaria purpurea* and *L. triornithophora*, *Verbena bonariensis*, and *Gaura lindheimeri*. These proletarians march on and provide good cheer for most of the year.

Since we started with insufficient water for a lawn and were too greedy to allow open spaces, the garden is basically congested, traversed by wheelbarrow-sized paths that curve about and do, indeed, provide many surprises around the next corner, often of plants unknown to the visitor.

We had hoped to be plantsmen as well as plant collectors; Lester once wrote, "The art of gardening consists in getting the plants to lie down together." I fear we often had to settle for less, and I can only hope that the exuberance of the plants themselves may compensate for the niceties and order we once hoped to achieve.

This dry, sunny slope centers around the rich red and yellow broom *Cytisus* 'Glory of Sunningdale', with a white toothbrush-flowered grevillea behind. In the far right background are two *Cytisus* 'Garnet', and down the slope are verbascums, *Armeria maritima*, dianthus, and achillea.

The large-branched echium with lavender flowers is a hybrid from several Canary Island species. Behind is the golden *Elaeagnus pungens* 'Maculata' and the red new growth of *Pieris formosa forrestii*. The flowering shrub to the right is *Leptospermum rotundifolium*.

Tall spikes of *Eremurus himalaicus* rise dramatically at the edge of the gray garden with its boxwood hedges and Italian oil jar. A stepped path to the house above passes an old Japanese yew, *Taxus cuspidata*, which was shaped successfully into topiary when already fully grown.

HOLLISTER HOUSE is a typical Connecticut saltbox, built around 1760, with some later additions. Most of the farm buildings have also survived — enormous barns and sheds and a hay moan, a two-and-a-half-story structure facing the house, from which a road used to lead to the hay fields on the hill above. These buildings form a small complex around a loosely defined courtyard. The main road used to pass right in front of the house, with the various outbuildings on either side of the road — the usual layout in the eighteenth century, when traffic was infrequent and slow-paced. The country road of today, however, is a far cry from the relatively quiet one of the eighteenth century, and we are fortunate that in the 1950s the previous owners had the road moved farther up the hill. Behind the house the land slopes gently down to a long pond. It is an unusual and beautiful setting, and it gave us many possibilities to consider.

When I studied landscape architecture at Cornell University, I found the prevailing ideas about garden design utterly repellent. I decided that rather than design the kidney-shaped pools and other such horrors so beloved by my professors, I would do better to paint the landscape, and eventually I earned my degree in fine arts instead of landscape architecture. I never lost my love of landscape, however, and in the years since I left Cornell my tastes have remained rooted in the English gardening tradition. (Now that English gardening has become practically a mania in the United States, I am pleased to note that the kidney is in sharp decline in the affections of American gardeners.)

Twelve years ago, when we were using Hollister House only as a weekend residence, there was no garden, just an attractive setting and a lovely old house with a leaky roof and holes in the walls. We devoted every available weekend to exploring the farm and assessing the house's most pressing needs — a new roof, new plumbing, and so on. Our vacations were spent in England marveling at the glorious private and public gardens there. We purchased books, took pictures and notes, and created a plan to integrate our fantasies with the limitations of our site. Particularly attractive to me were the possibilities afforded by the two streams that ran through the property; visions of pools and fountains danced through my head.

Our trips to England became frequent and taught us much. Each time we went, we came back home to America with hundreds of slides to comb for ideas. The names Jekyll, Robinson, Chatto, Hidcote, Great Dixter, and Sissinghurst became household words. We also shipped back decorative objects from England for the garden: a large copper laundry pot, a huge brass cheese vat, an old granite baluster supposedly taken from London Bridge, several three-foot-high rhubarb forcers, and an antique stone trough.

A view of the neighboring fields beyond the main lawn and the new garden house. On the other side of the brick wall is the main garden with its twelve-foot-deep borders and its twenty-eight-foot-long reflecting pool.

We were to have an English garden, and that is what we started to create, though in the end I think the result is very American. I see it as a composite of various influences, experiences, and information, all modified as necessary in relation to our particular circumstances in New England. We drew many designs and labored over an overall plan for the garden. Each of our fantasies included a series of garden rooms. Each new path suggested yet another vista, a resting place, sometimes even another garden. Plans were always being modified. We even built a three-dimensional clay model to give ourselves a better idea of how the garden would finally look.

Now, some eight or nine years later, the bulldozers are gone, the walls built, the paths laid — there is even a fountain. We prepared our canvas and have been painting on it with plants ever since. Each season and each year have brought with them hundreds of new varieties and species, variously given us by friends, ordered from catalogues, and on occasion collected from roadsides. Some I have grown since childhood and managed to bring in from my mother's garden. All of these exist side by side, woven into the tapestry of plants we have created here. This tapestry is always being ripped apart and remade according to the demands of the moment, as plants die, spread, and become unmanageable or just begin to bore.

For me the excitement of a new spring is always a joy. There are my old friends

The pale blush peony 'Mrs. Franklin D. Roosevelt' and the bright-pink self-sown *Silene armeria* figure prominently in this early June border in the main garden, along with *Salvia* 'Mainacht' and blue *Tradescantia virginiana*. In the foreground a large clump of the native American *Gillenia trifoliata* makes a mass of delicate white blossom behind a hybrid white dianthus.

the plants and my old enemies the diseases and the weeds. And then there are the special new recruits that we have nicknamed the R&Ds, short for Rare and Desirables. And it is true for me, as I have read it is for many gardeners, that my favorite flower is always the one in bloom. I suppose that makes me some kind of fair-weather friend.

To me one of the best effects in this garden comes in the spring, when a sheet of forget-me-nots creeps through the garden, and all from a fifty-cent packet of seed! Other effects are more costly, not only in money but also in time spent waiting and in the sheer labor of digging up the ground to enrich or replace the soil. A white redbud, *Cercis canadensis* 'Alba', which arrived as a promising whip, is now a small tree. In the spring its almost black bark is covered with white pearls; during the summer its pale, heart-shaped leaves form a canopy over the small octagonal garden near the house. Soon it will be big enough for its branches to be cut for bouquets.

New sets of problems arise, and by intention or by accident, new effects occur. The garden has started to mature, and best of all, some of the visions we had when we first saw those beautiful English gardens have evolved into reality.

RON JOHNSON

W E BOTH WANTED a formal garden, the old-fashioned kind with right angles and straight paths, with walls and hedges and big exuberant herbaceous borders—that much we were agreed upon. And we knew what we did not want, which was anything remotely reminiscent of the usual naturalistic style of suburban gardens, whose every line must be artfully curved and whose every flower must be the latest overblown hybrid—as if anything could look less natural than that. Nature herself, of course, can make breathtakingly beautiful garden pictures, but the man-made imitations I have almost always found disappointing. It takes an extremely talented gardener, someone who is also a first-rate artist, to be able to manage confidently and successfully the illusion of a natural garden. There is always something that gives the game away and cries fraud to the eye of any truly visual person. How much more sensible, then, to be honest about it and admit that it is all right for a garden to look like a garden, instead of like an enchanted glade or a woodland pond or whatever other flight of self-delusion the poor gardener may have fallen into.

I like to think of our garden as a thoroughly civilized environment, where nature has been tamed and harnessed for the pleasure of human beings. Now and then, however, I feel that nature should be given her head, as when she wants to sow her own seeds or when a plant decides to grow out of the bounds we have planned for it. In fact Ron and I both like a certain wildness in the way the garden is planted. There is something exciting, even a bit romantic, about a formal garden that is slightly overgrown. The key word here is *slightly*, since a romantic tangle of blossom can easily develop into a common, or garden-variety, mess if the gardener does not know when to step in and curb high spirits.

Eleven years ago, when we began to talk seriously about making our garden, we had just returned from a tour of English gardens. Instead of having a Sissinghurst to plan our garden around, however, we had only an eighteenth-century Connecticut farmhouse— pretty and charming, to be sure, but without the slightest pretension to grandeur or high

Broad granite steps provide an ideal environment for such low-growing plants as *Salvia officinalis* 'Nana' (upper right). The large blue-gray leaves of *Crambe maritima* contrast with the finer texture of the mass of yellow *Helianthemum nummularium* beneath. At center left is a neat clump of the deeper yellow *Hypericum olympicum minus*, and at top left, two viciously invasive but evenly matched opponents, *Oenothera fruticosa* and *Artemisia ludoviciana* 'Silver King', mount a striking late June display of bright-yellow blossom and brilliant silver foliage.

The main garden in full June dress. To the left, *Rosa moyesii* towers above the yew hedge and brick wall. The glaucous leaves and white flowers of *Crambe maritima* and a giant form of *Stachys byzantina* border the flagstone path, with the violet-blue *Campanula latiloba* adding color behind. A sang-de-boeuf Chinese jar echoes the color of the purple-leaved plum in the foreground and a purple-leaved form of *Cercis canadensis* 'Forest Pansy'.

style. We realized that there was a real danger of a large formal garden's seeming out of place in our simple country setting, and this we were determined to avoid.

Our solution, arrived at only after much disagreement and experimentation with one plan after another, was to site the main garden, with its eight-foot-high brick walls and its twenty-eight-foot-long reflecting pool, diagonal to the house so that the house is not on axis and can be glimpsed only casually from the garden. The other garden spaces we kept smaller and more in proportion to the house itself. We designed a progression of small gardens — or "rooms," as the English sometimes say — each separated from the next by a hedge, fence, or wall, and we took particular pains to create vistas from one space to and through the next one so that the eye would always be led on to some new surprise.

Our other major problem was how to terrace our sloping site, since the sort of garden we envisaged demanded flat spaces on which to lay out the paths and plant the borders and hedges. We were fortunate in having a neighbor who was a professional builder. He explained that the type of retaining wall we were planning to build would last two years at most before the hard New England frost heaved it down onto the main garden, and he offered to take charge of the construction. What we ended up with was a steel-reinforced concrete wall built to highway specifications, with footings six feet deep. This hideous fabrication—the other neighbors said it looked like a supermarket basement—we then

had faced in handmade brick that would be able to withstand our −20° winters. The final effect was so soft and mellow that one visitor asked if the wall had been the foundation of an old barn, a mistake that we took as a high compliment.

Throughout the ensuing years we have planted the garden with a variety of rare and common plants. We like to experiment with new plants and new plant combinations; if they do not work in one location we move them to another until we have achieved something satisfying. However, if I am to be entirely honest, I will have to admit that some of our greatest successes have happened quite by accident.

Gardening in this climate is always problematic, and often this year's triumph is next year's failure as disease or bad weather foils our best-laid plans. Lately I have found myself becoming more attracted to safer solutions, especially as the garden has expanded and there is so much more of it to tend. We are still discovering what the different plants can and cannot do, but little by little the garden is arriving at the comfortable maturity for which we have always been aiming.

GEORGE SCHOELLKOPF

The reflecting pool in June. The old roses 'Veilchenblau' and the Gallica rose 'Complicata' join forces with *Lonicera japonica* 'Halliana' to clothe the eight-foot retaining wall beneath the gray garden. *Geranium* 'Johnson's Blue' and *Alchemilla mollis* spill into the pool, with self-sown foxgloves and *Allium giganteum* behind. Annual white and deep-violet Japanese iris and miniature white gladioli will provide blossom through the months ahead. The pale spiked leaves on the right are *Acorus calamus* 'Variegatus'.

I HAVE OFTEN THOUGHT how few Americans today have the privilege of working in the same garden, using the same tools and techniques, as their grandparents. In my family, gardens, tools, techniques, and especially an intimate knowledge of the land and its management have been passed on through three generations. As it has aged, the garden has developed a comfortable and settled character.

It was my great-grandfather who began our tenancy here. In 1883 he purchased Hedgleigh, a gentleman's farm that took its name from the long Osage orange hedges, originally meant to confine livestock. The house at Hedgleigh Spring was built in 1909, down near the farm's old springhouse, by my grandfather William J. Cresson. He had just married, and along with raising a family he started to create a garden. On his death, in 1959, my father, William junior, took over, maintaining the place until my brother, Richard, and I developed an interest and began to help out.

It is a tranquil setting, with the cedar-shingled springhouse (preserved in its original form) nestling among a grove of towering white oak, black gum, and beech. My grandfather's house was built under the largest of these oaks, and growing from its huge trunk, fifteen feet in circumference, the branches shade much of the house today. Farther back on the property a small stream meanders across a meadow. As the farm gradually evolved into a comfortable suburban neighborhood, my grandfather retained nearly two acres for his developing gardens.

He must have had a grand vision. I do not know where his inspiration originated, but no doubt he was influenced by the many fine local gardens. Hedgleigh Spring is the last remaining example of those small early-twentieth-century flower gardens.

Photographs show that by the late 1920s my grandfather had established the layout for the various connecting garden areas. He constructed a series of gentle terraces and grade changes throughout the lower part of the property, cleverly disguised with trees and shrubs, and to achieve this built dry stone retaining walls up to four feet high and totaling more than a tenth of a mile. Included in his original design are more than a hundred feet of perennial borders, woodland gardens, a water garden, and a vegetable garden. It is remarkable that all of this work was done by my grandfather himself after the age of forty!

The roof garden on the front porch, with hen-and-chickens, sedum, and even the native prickly pear (*Opuntia humifusa*) growing on the moss-covered shingles, provides

A dry stone wall next to the lattice springhouse is tightly planted for a long season of bloom. Here, in light shade, *Pulmonaria saccharata* and *Alyssum saxatile* dominate the scene in April.

The sunken garden in June, from behind the white picket fence. The cool colors along the fence show well against the dark, shady background; the flowers include foxglove, astilbe, heuchera, *Lychnis coronaria*, *Silene armeria*, feverfew, and *Oenothera tetragona*.

The house was built in 1909 under the massive white oak on the left. Sempervivum and sedum grow in the moss on the roof of the front porch. The twelve-foot *Acer palmatum* var. *dissectum* in the center was originally planted at my great-grandfather's farmhouse nearly a hundred years ago.

The trellis bed in June displays original varieties from my grandfather's time. Period climbing roses from the early 1900s include white 'Silver Moon', pink 'Mary Wallace', and 'Paul's Scarlet Climber'. A new addition, the small-flowered *Clematis* 'Etoile Violette', clambers over them. Other original varieties include heuchera, cottage pinks, foxgloves, and, in the foreground, many of the Hybrid Tea roses.

a hint of what is to follow. But the prevailing atmosphere is one of quiet grandeur as the oaks tower over the lawn surrounding the house, bordered by mature azaleas and rhododendrons. The prominent Japanese cutleaf maple (*Acer palmatum* var. *dissectum*), with twisted branches exceeding twelve feet, was moved here from the old farmhouse.

Passing through an azalea border behind the house, visitors are always surprised when they enter the sunken garden, where several low steps lead down into a flower garden of perennials and roses bordering a spacious lawn. Carved out of a gentle slope, the sunken area is enhanced by side walls backed by raised flower beds. At the far end, a pair of curved perennial borders is backed by a ninety-one-foot-long semicircular white picket fence. It is a truly unique innovation of my grandfather's—I know of no other example of a picket fence erected in a half circle.

In June the sunken garden reaches its peak, with perennials and biennials bursting out in a medley of textures and colors. On the side, old climbing roses such as white 'Silver Moon' and pink 'Mary Wallace' clamber over a trellis along with the small-flowered purple *Clematis* 'Etoile Violette'. Tall foxgloves, *Silene armeria*, heuchera, and cottage pinks cluster in front of the trellis. The two curved beds along the picket fence have separate color schemes to avoid basic clashes. The sunny side is planted with hot reds, oranges, and yellows, and the shadier side has cooler pinks, whites, and mauves, brightened with pale yellow and a touch of red, all against a dark background. Asters, Japanese

In the woodland gardens, white pine and hemlock shelter a rich understory of shrubs and herbaceous plants. Contrasting foliages lend interest to this tranquil setting even in winter. Here, the June bloom of an old rhododendron hybrid, which will be followed in July by the flowers of this orange form of plumleaf azalea (*Rhododendron prunifolium*, center) and lavender spikes of *Hosta crispula*.

anemones, kniphofias, and many others sustain the sunken garden's display through the end of September.

The sunken garden is the center of the property, its very heart. The design of the rest revolves around the unique shape of this garden and its curved fence, inviting further exploration. During the heat of summer, visitors eagerly seek refuge under tall conifers nearby, where a cool woodland character unites several garden rooms. In the English manner, rhododendrons and azaleas share space with several species of lace-cap hydrangeas, such as *H. serrata* and *H. aspera*, and at their feet exotic epimediums, trillium, arisaema, gingers (asarum), and many other herbaceous woodlanders inhabit the pine-needle mulch.

A focal point here is the toolhouse—originally an outhouse on the old farm—from which an array of paths lead to other gardens. Following one of these, one comes to a gate opening into the pond garden. This is truly a sunken garden, surrounded on three sides by stone walls and on the fourth by a bank, or dike, that gives protection against the nearby stream's flash floods during summer storms. Atop this bank, our native Atlantic white cedar, *Chamaecyparis thyoides*, makes a perfect clipped hedge, the only one of its kind I have ever seen, ideal because it retains its low branches so readily. In May the front of this bank is covered with a rainbow of polyanthus, just as it was sixty years ago. One variety, an antique gold laced polyanthus, has survived here for decades.

The bones of the pond garden remain as my grandfather left them. Photographs show that the small pond, gravity-fed by an underground pipe running from above the waterfall in the stream, just out of sight, was well established by the 1920s. Today, however, the plantings are richer and more diverse. At water's edge the pond is surrounded by masses of lovely white Japanese skunk cabbage (*Lysichiton camtschatcense*), candelabra primroses (*Primula japonica*, *P. pulverulenta*, *P.* x *bullesiana*), Japanese irises, forget-me-nots, and majestic cardinal flowers, blooming in turn as the season progresses. A carmine-pink waterlily, *Nymphaea* 'Gloriosa', flowers successfully in the somewhat shady conditions imposed by surrounding tall trees. Blue pickerel weed (*Pontederia cordata*) also thrives here, rising out of the water near the bank.

September is a pleasant surprise in the pond garden. Early in the month, the reds and blues of summer promptly fade. Raised beds above the walls come into bloom with the pinks of large crocuslike colchicums, sprays of pealike flowers of *Lespedeza thunbergii*, *Sedum spectabile*, and *Cyclamen hederifolium*. Lavender-blue *Crocus speciosus* and golden-yellow *Sternbergia lutea* follow in October, providing an engaging prelude to spring.

Another path from the toolhouse leads down three steps into the fern dell and the meadow beyond. The fern dell is another cleverly constructed sunken garden. Low walls surround the long woodland walk, secluded by familiar rhododendrons, azaleas, and hydrangeas. During my grandfather's time these walls enclosed a lawn, but the increased shade mandated a change, and today large native and exotic ferns line the path, enlivened by the contrasting foliage of lungwort, creeping *Phlox stolonifera*, and Solomon's seal.

The fern dell opens out to the stream with its dam and waterfall. The dam had been broken down by frost over the years and was restored in 1985; it not only supplies water for the pond but also serves as a bridge to the perennial meadow beyond.

First inspired ten or fifteen years ago by the vanishing fields and countryside, the meadow lends a suggestion of wilderness and seclusion along the back of the garden. At the height of summer, yellow *Silphium perfoliatum* and pink *Eupatorium purpureum* tower overhead. Later, tall perennial *Helianthus giganteus* stems lean down to eye-level with their clusters of small lemon-yellow sunflowers, followed by golden *H. angustifolius* to highlight the autumn colors in early November. Before winter comes, we cut

the meadow to discourage woody plants and to leave a clean slate for the spring bulbs.

Early in the new year the meadow comes alive with a carpet of snowdrops and *Crocus tomasinianus*, followed by thousands of daffodils, most of them smaller-flowered, old-fashioned hybrids from the 1800s. In April this mass of blooms is a major feature, visible even from the house. Later, drifts of star of Bethlehem (*Ornithogalum umbellatum*), Spanish wood hyacinths (*Hyacinthoides hispanica*), and native *Camassia leichtlinii* bloom among *Phlox divaricata*. The meadow is seldom without interest!

Few major changes have been made to the garden since my grandfather's time. The use of space and the placement of lawns, flower beds, trees, and shrubs are essentially untouched, as we attempt to preserve the character and style of this period garden. Within this framework, however, many areas have been rejuvenated and planted more intensively: the collection has grown to over two thousand varieties. In new perennial plantings, in both sun and shade, we have tried to create foliage compositions that provide lasting seasonal effect and enhance the fleeting bloom of each component.

The surface of the pond, surrounded by moisture-loving plants including astilbe, Japanese iris, and candelabra primroses, is broken in June by *Nymphaea* 'Gloriosa' and *Iris laevigata* 'Variegata'. To the left, on higher ground, are *Crambe cordifolia* and the white thistle, *Onopordum nervosum*, with *Clematis* 'Madame Edouard André' and *Rosa* 'Tausenschön' in the back.

The stone springhouse was part of my great-grandfather's farm at Hedgleigh and is at least 150 years old. My grandfather planted the dogwood, and my father and I planted the variegated pachysandra to brighten this dark corner.

Unfinished areas have been developed. Behind the house, a new winter border backed by evergreens is visible from the kitchen window. Fragrant *Osmanthus armatus*, *Galanthus reginae-olgae*, and hardy *Camellia oleifera* hybrids flower in October and November. Early bulbs and hellebores contribute to late-winter color, along with *Mahonia japonica*, witch hazel (*Hamamelis* 'Pallida'), Korean rhododendron (*Rhododendron mucronulatum*), and winter hazel (*Corylopsis* 'Winterthur'). For summer bloom, a new brick patio displays a changing assortment of potted bulbs and subtropicals. This tropical effect is enhanced by a vigorous banana, *Musa basjoo*, which is root-hardy here against the foundation of the house and grows annually to nine feet. Bold accents add excitement!

Responsibility for Hedgleigh Spring is gradually being taken over by the third generation. My brother, Richard, an adept mechanic and craftsman, and I, a professional horticulturist trained in England and America, still rely on the experienced assistance of our father. At times it is a daunting task that keeps us all hustling, but to us it is more than just a garden—it is a family heirloom.

Albert Richard Lamb III

GARDENING HAS BECOME MY AVOCATION, a pleasure reached through my profession, landscape architecture, though it was not until I owned a house that I began to enjoy the art of gardening. This was after completing two degree programs and living and traveling in Italy and France, which gave me the opportunity to steep myself in the history of garden design.

My wife, Nancy, and I arrived on the Cape in 1972, after studying for several years at the American Academy in Rome and working with Dan Kiley in Paris. Having amassed a huge reservoir of images and ideas, I embarked on a career as a landscape architect. We were lured to Barnstable by the ocean coast, the village landscape, its proximity to Boston, and the career opportunities it afforded. Our choice was reinforced when we discovered that several of our ancestors were early residents of the community.

Soon after our arrival, I recognized two cardinal features of Cape Cod. First, the Atlantic Ocean is the dominant force determining its climate. The Gulf Stream runs near the peninsula, and so the Cape enjoys a hardiness zone comparable to Virginia's. The inland palette of plants is broadened significantly here to include additional varieties of rhododendron, buxus, ilex, and prunus, as well as a wider range of herbs. The sea temperature also extends the summer well into the fall, creating a longer growing season. However, spring is much delayed, arriving two or three weeks later than in Boston. Additionally, the ocean winds affect the height of plants, creating a landscape with a lower profile than that found inland. My second observation relates to scale: buildings in many of the Cape's seaside communities are constructed at half to three-quarter height. Both of these things, the humanized scale and the rich and abundant combination of textures, create a wonderfully romantic environment.

Our house is a historic full Cape cottage, built around 1725 from traditional materials, with a stone foundation and an oak frame sheathed in wide pine boards and clad with naturally weathered cedar shingles. It is adjacent to an active farm on the north side of Cape Cod, facing south within a rolling rural landscape and planted with mature specimens. Our long, narrow half-acre, though formerly owned by a horticulturist, had only a few specimen survivors from what was once no doubt a lovely garden. A hint of good bones was implicit beneath the thickets. A field adjoined the house on the west side, and on the south there was the stone foundation of a small barn. Except for worn paths through the grasses, the house sat in an overgrown landscape.

I approached the creation of the garden very much as a landscape architect, not as a gardener. I formed the armature of the garden's design by extending the house's internal organization outward, creating garden rooms as extensions of interior spaces.

The public space, open to the street, is green on green, with no color accents save

Sculptural chamaecyparis and *Prunus laurocerasus* define the entrance and separate it from the garden, where the midsummer show of scabiosa, dianthus, late iris, and delphinium make pleasing bouquets, both indoors and out. The wisteria that bloomed after ten years has given us great pleasure.

for modest seasonal foliage change. The semiprivate space leads to the entrance between architecturally pruned masses of both evergreen and deciduous plants. The private space opens into rooms of varying sizes and moods, devoted to entertainment, relaxation, herbaceous beds, lawn, and loose, naturalized beds as transition to the agricultural landscape beyond. Apart from the overall green palette, color does not occur until one enters the private garden areas.

I have tried to make the most of this small garden by incorporating distant views while at the same time creating a great variety of private experiences. We felt it was important to do this through the use of native materials, thus preserving the Cape's historic integrity without suburbanizing its landscape. Exotic plants are reserved for the interior of the garden.

The inherited "bones" have matured nicely, each nurtured into its desired shape and function. Dominant are the trees—a very old apple tree, several mature maples, *Acer platanoides*, dogwoods, *Cornus florida* and *C. kousa*, mature lilac, *Syringa vulgaris*, and a pair of unusually large honeysuckle "trees." A giant Niobe willow tree, *Salix* x *pendulina* 'Blanda', is the majestic sentinel for the garden, and also serves as an accurate barometer of perfect sailing weather. The locust tree, *Gleditsia triacanthos*, became a marvelous umbrella over a kitchen terrace, letting through just the right amount of dappled morning sunlight. Two large winged euonymus bushes, *Euonymus alatus*, were treated in contrasting manner. The specimen immediately off the kitchen terrace was clipped architecturally to echo and extend the form of the small garden toolshed; the dense branching maintains the effect even after the bush has lost its leaves. The other one is kept low but allowed to assume the natural form of the species, providing a transition from the clipped garden to the fields beyond.

We also added plants to make the connection with the neighboring broad agricultural landscape. We defined the drive with a line of semidwarf apples, crop trees that are generally associated with the orchard but that when pleached become formal domestic specimens. Several varieties were chosen, to supply blossom and fruit over an extended period, and

The espaliered apple tree shares a support with a clothesline hung from the toolshed. Russian sage provides a good filler for arrangements well into the fall, and bee balm (*Monarda didyma*), while a fast-spreading nuisance, regularly attracts hummingbirds.

these are maintained at a height of ten feet, in keeping with the scale of the house. Beach plum, *Prunus maritima*, a native bush producing a tart fruit, terminates the drive. Creating an edge for the garden in summer, this deciduous plum becomes transparent in winter, allowing filtered views into the garden. The raspberries under the apples, along with the beach plum and some trodding herbs, present a wonderful sequence along the drive to the popular kitchen door.

We used buxus to form rooms within the overall garden structure. Many of the young boxwood were started by Nancy's mother, Helen Stutsman, an active member of the St. Louis Boxwood Society. These hedges extend the architecture, defining the intimate spaces nearest the house. The contrast between the beds and terraces and the broad landscape that opens out across the garden reflects the difference between Italian and French gardens. Even in a small area it is possible to create a dynamic contrast between manicured garden and natural landscape by borrowing from the horizon.

The gentle slope of the land gave us the opportunity to use bedding areas to the full through terracing. The terraces in effect extend both the house and the footprint of the former barn. Brick terraces were located to take advantage of sun and shade throughout the day, and to provide vistas of the immediate garden and the distant fields. The morning sun filters onto the terrace to the east, while those to the west provide wonderful niches for the warmth of the afternoon sun slanting over the fields.

As the garden structure matures, I find myself assuming the role of gardener. My interest now focuses on the composition of species and the joy of nurturing various plants and associations of plants. I take great pleasure in balancing the finer textures and colors. The true challenge has been to stretch the flowering time of the garden: I now record the last blue vinca between Thanksgiving and Christmas and celebrate our first snowdrop in the beginning of February. Early spring on the Cape is first appreciated through little things. The ground turns blue with chionodoxa, crocus, and muscari when tree frogs begin their early-evening chirping, and a broad mix of daffodils and narcissus follows. I have overplanted the bulbs with hostas so that the dying bulb foliage is hidden by the emerging hosta leaves.

Spring and early summer seem to present the gentlest blooms, with border plants of wood geranium, iberis, and daphne. I am presently experimenting with varieties of iris— *Iris sibirica* and *I. ensata* (*kaempferi*)—that blend well with the later-blooming belamcanda and serve as skirts for the delphiniums, liatris, astilbe, and lythrum. The garden bordering the driveway supplies not only our vegetables but also cut flowers from summer to fall.

The most difficult and perhaps the most rewarding aspect of our garden is that we are in Barnstable only on weekends. The challenge has been to develop the proper soil with sufficient drainage to sustain reasonable plant growth. When we first prepared the beds, many bales of salt-marsh hay and peat moss were worked into the existing clay, and the combination has produced a well-insulated and well-balanced soil, on which I rely to protect the garden during the week, as each growing season can be extremely varied.

The overall balance of the garden has given us great pleasure. During late spring, summer, and early fall, when we are outside a great deal, it becomes enclosed by its own greenery, and we enjoy wonderful privacy. As the leaves fall and we move indoors, the rolling fields outside combine with the more immediate garden to expand our realm.

I am pleased to be recognized by others as a gardener; the implication of knowledge is flattering, and the rewards are great. As a designer, I must ensure that my plans reflect the conditions, programs, and personalities of others. In our own garden, I am creating for our personal pleasure and for the pleasure of our friends.

The silver herb garden features santolina, sage, silver mound, artemisia, lamb's ears, and lavender. The trodding herbs, which do not survive our winters, are planted annually; their subtle fragrance makes the effort worthwhile.

THE GARDEN OF

Kevin M. Nicolay

QUEEN ANNE HILL, SEATTLE, WASHINGTON

THE HEART OF THE CITY of Seattle is built on a necklace of hills that ring Elliott Bay, a cul-de-sac in Puget Sound. One of these hills, Queen Anne, rises between the shores of the bay and Lake Union, a freshwater lake set in the expanding city. Cut off from most of the major city thoroughfares, Queen Anne Hill remains a quiet, green neighborhood of old houses and small apartment buildings. I made my present garden on the eastern face of the hill, on land overlooking the lake and with an unobstructed view of the sunrise; the small lot had been carved out of the slope like a stair riser.

The house is a typical 1920s Seattle bungalow, built, as is common here, high up from the street. A steep flight of steps rises from the sidewalk to the front door, and on either side of this is a concrete bed raised to about my chest height (I am six feet tall) and canted out and downward from the house at its end. In addition to these two awkward attachments, which require me either to climb over the porch or get out a ladder to garden them, there is a narrow bed separating my driveway from my neighbor's land below.

The soil in the immediate vicinity is straight sand, and the southern orientation of the house makes the little front garden hot and dry, a rare commodity in these parts. The odd construction of the bulkhead attachments, which allows water to run off rather than sink in, makes it impossible to water with anything other than the most timid of soaker hoses. Rather than fight this situation, as most of my neighbors do, I decided that this was my chance to exercise my dormant love of Mediterranean plants.

In the tilted fronts of the high beds I planted a tapestry of drought-tolerant things with gold and silver leaves: thyme, dwarf and woolly lavender, curious Grecian oreganos with pendant hop flowers, *Crambe maritima*, verbascums, and phlomis. To offset the self-satisfied roundness of some of these, I added the vertical fountain of *Kniphofia galpinii* and the blue-leaved, aloe-trunked *K. caulescens*, as well as golden-variegated yuccas and the stiff and bristly *Acanthus spinosus*. I put *Cytisus battandieri* and two *Rosa foetida* 'Bicolor', or Austrian copper roses, into the bed between my driveway and my neighbor's; this narrow area is the driest of the three beds, and the rose responds to the parched conditions with lack of black spot and with more intensely colored flowers.

Taking further advantage of the baking southern exposure and enforced drought, I packed all three beds with bulbs in a catholic array. Into the eye-level tapestries went all the little iris, crocus, and hoop-petticoat daffodils that needed close inspection; it became a delight to go out in winter and look a dozen *Iris reticulata* cultivars, *Bulbocodium vernum*, and a host of miffy little daffodils straight in the eye. At the foot of the roses I made a Persian enamel with species tulips, Onocyclus iris, the mysterious little green

Clockwise from upper left:

Roscoea 'Beesiana', a hardy member of the ginger family, bears orchidlike flowers in midsummer. It also has the unlooked-for benefit of distinctive foliage, which contrasts well with surrounding low "round" plants.

Decoration for one corner of the brick paving: *Ruta graveolens* 'Jackman's Blue' contrasts with a little-known variation on basket-of-gold (*Alyssum saxatile*) called 'Dudley Nevill Variegated'.

Two companions for a dry spot: after flowering, *Thymus praecox arcticus minus* provides a rich green background for the lengthening hop flowers of *Origanum pulchellum*, a decorative oregano.

The blue, succulent leaves of *Crambe maritima* 'Lily White' are veiled in the greenery-yallery of *Bupleurum falcatum*.

hermodactylus, anemones, arums, and seven different forms of *Iris unguicularis*. From what could have been a gardener's nightmare, I now pick glassfuls of iris buds to open indoors.

With the summer's baking, the sharp drainage, and nearby bodies of water to temper winter weather, I found I could grow plants that failed for others. That scintillating bindweed *Convolvulus cneorum* spangled itself with blossoms every May, defying the doomsayers who assured me it would not last. In a protected corner, *Olearia macrodonta*, the New Zealand daisy bush, prospers in rude health, and various unusual low hebes spill out along with the thyme and lavender. *Solanum crispum* 'Glasnevin' scales the porch, but it has a mind of its own: the summer's dryness seems to frustrate its attempts to produce the crop of autumn flowers it is famous for, so it delays until spring, massing its campanula-violet potato blossoms with the soft apricot of the rose 'Alchimist'. (My best associations are often the ones I cannot take credit for.)

Despite all of my individual plant successes here, I faced the continuing aggravation of having to try to tie the house and all its bare concrete to the ground. Its exaggerated height made it stare down in a bald sort of way, and the narrow beds left little room for the Italian cypress and Russian olive that would have, in my opinion, finished the picture off. Denied the scale I wanted, I took to knocking holes in the sidewalk at the base of the bulkhead and masking some of their faces with cistus, the broom 'Pink Spot', *Rosa primula*, and *Carpenteria californica*. Here, in front of these walls, I have one of my greatest triumphs: *Daphne genkwa* flourishes and wreathes itself in lilac flowers. Covering the porch with the vines mentioned earlier helped, as did letting *Euphorbia characias wulfenii*, *Lobelia*

The front porch is swathed in a stole of 'Alchimist', a rose that is not only lavish in flowering but also excellent on poor soil and in other difficult spots.

laxiflora, and *Halimium lasianthum* spill down the face of the raised beds to meet the plants that grew up from below. I made a few mistakes, planting things that overstepped their bounds—a *Senecio* 'Sunshine' with pretensions to empire, for instance, and a lavender that would not obey the law of gravity, refusing to cascade.

While the front garden has been an occasional source of annoyance to me, the back garden has given me nothing but pleasure. It is a perfect secret garden, a little *hortus conclusus* out of a medieval manuscript, protected on two sides by tall retaining walls (which keep the neighbors above from dropping in unexpectedly after a rainstorm) and screened by a crown of small trees, hedges, and ivy, as well as a fence. On the third side is the north wall of the house, with a cool deck from which I can admire my work in summer, and on the fourth side the garden is open to the immediate rise of the sun as it clears the next hill. Consequently, rather than being a shady retreat, as one might expect of a town garden, the space is filled with light, warm and sheltered, and in it the old roses I love open a full three weeks earlier than do those in the rest of the city.

Though not as small as the present one, all of my previous gardens were restricted in land, and I came to tackle this little space with a clear idea of what a small garden should be. I wanted a representative selection of the abundance that botany was capable of, so that when I stood in the middle of the garden I would feel as though I were at the bottom of a well of flowers. At the same time I knew that, denied the advantage of vistas and borrowed views, I would have to lead the eye inward. One of the best ways to accomplish this was by using unusual plants: a border of the unexpected makes one stop and draw closer, requiring a second and third look to identify and admire.

Before I could plant anything in the back garden, however, I had to "clear the land" by removing a jumble of unsuitable trees and shrubs, as well as a handyman's garden ornament in the form of a brick barbecue grill. After I had dispatched the grill with a sledgehammer and removed extraneous plants, I prepared the soil. Over the course of the first year I poured thirty yards of organic material into the ground, making use of composted wood and poultry bedding, cow manure, chicken manure, and "Zoo-do"—a product of the animals at Seattle's Woodland Park Zoo. After all this attention, the beds were nearly three feet high and very suspicious-looking. One friend asked whether it had taken one bottle of poison or two to do in all my relatives so quickly.

While the beds settled, I went about acquiring plants—more than could ever have fitted in comfortably. I sent off for new hostas, American natives, cultivars of herbaceous plants I had never heard of, daylilies, peonies. I brought back plants from my old garden in Ohio, was given lovely things by friends, and enthusiastically ordered perennials and roses from England.

I made a lot of mistakes. I fell for the luscious catalogue descriptions in the worst way and was frequently disappointed, as when the rose that was supposed to be "richest vinous purple" turned out to be a harsh pink, and the "near-white" daylily a dull beige. In my rush to grow all sorts of new things, I often turned a blind eye to sizes given for particular plants. I also tried to make plant associations from the enticing words in the catalogues, only to find out that things bloomed differently in Seattle.

I think I have been rewarded for all my preparation, acquisition, and plant moving by the well of flowers that I set out to make and now enjoy. The year starts early, with snowdrops and black *Helleborus orientalis*, which I raise and hybridize, followed by all of the foliage—rodgersias, pulmonarias, ferns, hostas—along with the early blooms of species peonies. The garden is at its most refulgent in June, when the old roses I have selected outdo themselves in flower. At one end the thornless Boursault rambler 'Amadis' spills

In order to raise interest from ground-level and provide some much-needed verticality, tripods are covered with various climbers. Here the rose 'Sombreuil' is wrapped over its support and accompanied by *Campanula latiloba*, *Artemisia ludoviciana latifolia* (syn. *A.* 'Valerie Finnis'), and *Salvia* 'Mainacht'.

Although I try for almost year-round interest, I admit to succumbing to the month of June, when my favorites, the old roses, cover themselves in glory.

down the wall into a cottage garden I am making on donated land, and at the other that inestimable climber 'Paul's Lemon Pillar' leans on a tripod covered in 'Sombreuil', each of them making for a more enclosed feeling without taking up as much space as a small tree might. Over a small pergola shared with a venerable grapevine there is 'Ash Wednesday', modern in introduction but antique in shape and coloring, its lilac flowers harmonizing perfectly with *Clematis* 'Silver Moon'. Amid the herbaceous plants are some of the smaller shrub roses, my favorite being an old crimson and purple 'Hybrid Perpetual' that came under the name 'Rose du Roi à Fleur Pourpre'. I am assured by several rosarian friends that it is not that at all, but I pay this no mind; it is too sumptuously constructed and scented for me to worry much about its nomenclature.

After the roses and their companions have finished, the garden takes a short breath and then breaks out into full summer. Agapanthus, selected for their deepest blue, rise amid the frosty leaves of *Crambe maritima* and *Iris pallida* 'Aureo-variegata', veiled in a cloud of the acid-yellow, dill-like foliage of a little-known English wildflower, *Bupleurum falcatum*. Against a backdrop of artemisias and the blue of *Melianthus major*, *Phlox* 'Norah Leigh' rises above *Kniphofia* 'Little Maid'. To a scene that is predominantly blue and yellow in summer, I added the soft pink of *Lavatera thuringiaca* 'Rosea' for its mass and long flowering, and some double pink and white Japanese anemones to carry on into autumn. When September approaches, the deep purple of *Clematis* 'Lady Betty Balfour'

decorates the lavatera. Through this the stunning black-eyed, plum-magenta flowers of *Geranium* 'Anne Folkard' weave on long trailing stems, blooming right through until frost. This particular geranium has won my admiration, and I now find I would not want to be without it.

My garden owes a great deal of its success to the qualities of mystery and surprise. The approach from front to back is down a cool and leaf-canopied corridor—a result of the fact that the house and retaining walls run parallel to each other. At the end of this tunnel is an arch of ivy through which one must pass before the garden is revealed. I have tried further to enhance this buildup through my choice of plants, placing the roses so that they partially block what grows behind them, veiling the whole area from immediate view with a scrim of crambe and thalictrum.

I have made what some might call a mistake, putting all my eggs in a herbaceous basket in order to make the most of spring, summer, and autumn and their abundance. With the exception of a fine umbrella pine and the ivy that rings the walls, there is little winter interest here. In December, January, and February, the garden and I both lie fallow; over the dark wet days I forget what riches are buried there and what secrets the empty ground is keeping. I forget until some warm night in early March, when that tender and imperturbable green steals over every inch of the garden, powerfully keeping the old promise. To me this is the most riveting mystery and the very best surprise of all.

July advances with a favorite clematis, 'Perle d'Azur', rising above a surrounding border of foliage and flowers. The plants include *Phlox paniculata* 'Norah Leigh', *Crambe maritima*, *Verbascum chaixii*, and *Lychnis coronaria oculata*.

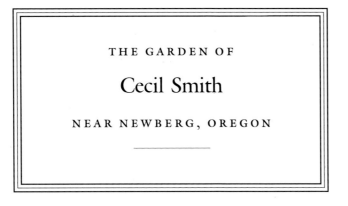

I AM ONE OF THOSE FORTUNATE GARDENERS who, having developed a great love for one kind of plant—in my case, rhododendrons—found the ideal place for them to thrive.

My garden is on a north-facing slope shaded by a grove of Douglas firs, just a few miles east of the family farmhouse where I was born. Near that farmhouse was an area where the trees had been cut; in the spring the wildflowers would spring up among the limbs, stumps, and logs on the ground. There were yellow violets, our small wild *Iris tenax*, trilliums, and dodecatheons. I liked those fresh, young, green plants better than the well-cared-for flowers in my parents' garden.

I am sure those childhood memories influenced our choice of the five wooded acres that have become our garden, and all of those small woodland plants I loved as a child grow here now. This slope was logged in 1915, but the fir trees had grown up again by 1951, when we bought the property and started building our house on the high ground on the south side of the slope. Almost all of the garden stretches out below the large windows on the north side of the house.

I began moving the first rhododendrons in before the house was finished. Paths were laid out across the slope, leaving stumps in place and moss-covered logs where they lay. Wild huckleberry grew in some of the logs, and I added other vacciniums and gaultherias. In one stump *Kalmiopsis leachiana* finds the perfect drainage it requires, and in other old stumps rhododendrons and trilliums have seeded themselves.

Not only was the site ideal for growing rhododendrons, but I was also particularly lucky in the choice of a microclimate. The dark-brown forest duff is fifteen inches deep over a good soil; the fir trees provide moving shade and protection on the east and west sides; the slope allows cold air to drain away; and the small mountains that rise between the garden and Portland, thirty miles to the east, serve as a barrier against the severely cold wind that often blows down the Columbia Gorge.

The climate of the Willamette Valley in western Oregon is somewhat similar to that of southeastern England. Total rainfall is about forty inches a year, though there is very little rain from June to September. There are about fifteen days when the temperature rises over 90°, and a few days when it may drop below 10°.

Grafted hybrids, such as 'Pink Pearl', were the most readily available rhododendrons when we began, but they have now all been removed from the garden because after a number of years they began to develop problems at the graft union. Loderi 'King George',

The woodland garden in spring. Separating rhododendrons that flower at the same time makes color combinations easier to control.

To the left is a group of thirty *Rhododendron yakushimanum* 'Koichiro Wada' seedlings, with several more dwarfs to the right of the path, among *Anemone nemorosa*. A large 'Koichiro Wada' FCC mother plant grows under a golden chain tree. There are fields beyond the fir trees to the north.

Bergenia purpurascens, from southeastern Tibet, is an interesting foliage plant with dark-green spatulate leaves and pink flowers. It is hardy here and blooms profusely for a long period.

growing on its own roots, is the oldest and largest rhododendron, a mass of fragrant white flowers in May. 'Ibex' is planted where the afternoon sun will shine through its red flowers. 'Sir Charles Lemon', now fifteen feet tall, is admired for the undersides of its leaves, which are covered with cinnamon indumentum, a woolly covering found on some rhododendron leaves.

The hybrid rhododendrons could go directly into the forest soil, but as my interest turned more to species rhododendrons, I discovered that they did better if the soil was raised by the addition of leafmold, or barkdust and sawdust, which I kept in piles to age, plus a small amount of commercial fertilizer. In a year or so, when the plants become established, they look better without any fertilizer; it tends to make them fat and droopy, and to decrease the natural variation in leaf size and color that is one of the major attractions of the species.

The needs of the various rhododendron species are widely different. The original habitat for a dwarf rhododendron may have been a gravelly slope above the tree line, but the larger rhododendrons may have been small trees themselves, in a mixed forest thousands of feet lower down. My first consideration when choosing a planting site is the amount of sun or shade it receives. Then I try to group the rhododendrons that require less water. Although larger rhododendrons are generally planted toward the back, the size of their leaves compared to those of nearby plants is also considered. Since I prefer not to have adjacent plants blooming at the same time, I have not needed to give much thought to color combinations.

I like to grow some of the more vigorous species, including my favorite, *R. falconeri,* limbed-up as trees, with the bark exposed to show the interesting variations it has when mature. Providing contrast, three *Acer griseum* planted together have peeling, golden-brown bark, *Betula utilis jacquemontii* displays dazzling white bark, and *Prunus serrulata* is covered with shining mahogany bark.

Rising above the rhododendrons are *Prunus* 'Tai-haku', the largest-flowered of the Japanese cherries, and the Japanese umbrella pine, *Sciadopitys verticillata.* Near the bottom of the garden is a rare Chinese tree, *Rehderodendron macrocarpum,* whose racemes of white flowers are a reminder of its relationship to styrax. Here also, where the wind will not damage their big leaves, are *Rhododendron rex fictolacteum, R. falconeri eximium, R. montroseanum,* and *R. macabeanum.*

Our native inside-out flower (*Vancouveria hexandra*) and wild ginger (*Asarum caudatum*) cover the ground, and with encouragement, the pink dogtooth violet, *Erythronium revoltum,* makes a twenty-foot square. A single plant of white *Anemone deltoidea,* found in our woods, has spread over a large area since all nearby competition has been kept at a distance. *Jeffersonia diphylla, Tanakaea radicans,* and various species of trillium grow between the rhododendrons, while *Cardiocrinum giganteum,* the majestic Himalayan lily, soars six feet above.

I think a plant in a woodland garden should grow as it wants, with as little watering, fertilizing, and pruning as possible, though timeliness is still important in cultivating, planting, and weeding. Unless a woodland garden is weeded, it is not a garden — it is a wild area.

As my garden has matured, my favorite tool has been an ax. I do not like plants to be crowded and believe it is better to eliminate one plant than to prune back several.

With so many trees around, limbs keep coming down, especially in winter, but I never haul anything away. I think the wild effect of a woodland garden is enhanced if the limbs and leaves are left where they drop, though the biggest limbs are cut into pieces and

A woodland garden scene showing various rhododendrons that bloom from March to June. The rich forest soil and the sheltering fir trees create a perfect microclimate for them.

tucked under the larger rhododendrons to return nourishment to the soil. I always work some of my aged barkdust into the soil before planting a rhododendron, but for the dwarf rhododendrons I like to line the planting hole with two inches of leafmold. By the time the roots grow through the leafmold, the barkdust in the surrounding soil has begun to rot.

West of the house is a quarter of an acre with a canopy of wild hazelnut bushes. Under these I planted several species of trillium and each year continued to scatter seeds of cyclamen and erythronium. The hazelnuts provide summer shade, and their fallen leaves nourish the bulbs. It has been a very successful combination, providing a dense carpet of spring bloom with no care at all.

Rhododendrons that have heavy indumentum on their leaves are my favorites. Growing on a rotten stump, *R. proteoides,* whose tiny leaves have a two-layered indumentum below, flowered for the first time in cultivation in this garden. I enjoyed a worldwide correspondence with people writing for pollen from my *R. yakusimanum,* which was one of the first of its species to bloom outside of Japan. I was also interested in crossing *R. yakusimanum* with other species, especially those that also had indumentum. Some of these hybrids, including 'Noyo Chief' and 'Cinnamon Bear', turned out to be outstanding foliage plants.

As the garden became better known, garden clubs and individual gardeners wanted to visit along with the rhododendron fanciers, sometimes by the busload. When my wife, Molly, and I realized that we needed to garden on a smaller scale, we wished to preserve the place but still keep it available for study and public visits, so we made it possible for the Portland chapter of the American Rhododendron Society to acquire the garden.

CREATING A GARDEN in this southeastern area of New York State is often a challenge fraught with physical obstacles: massive granite boulders and out-crops, poor and shallow soil, forests of hardwood, and other trees and shrubs producing dense shade. These precise features confronted my wife, Esta, and me when we purchased our home and its surrounding rocky woodlands in April 1937. The one-and-a-half-acre property is located in an established suburban town in Westchester County, bordering Long Island Sound.

The temperature ranges from a dependable 0° and below in winter to near 100° at the peak of summer—a spread of a hundred degrees, twice that of most areas of England. In severe winters, sustained frigid weather without substantial snow may result in a terrain frozen two feet deep, a condition that is highly damaging to many plants. Summers present the opposite extremes of possible drought or excessive rain with humid and tropical heat—the scourge of alpines and other cool-climate flora. But woodland shade tempers the severity of each season, reducing summer heat and delaying autumn frost, sometimes into December.

We planned to develop this irregular terrain in three stages, half an acre at a time. The first area to be tackled was the rocky outcrop surrounding the house, where some trees and shrubs had already been cleared. The major challenge was to place suitable large rocks found in our adjacent woodland in such a way as to supplement existing shallow outcrops and to provide entrance steps up the slope to the house. Most of these were bedded inconspicuously in cement, and a series of cascading pools of native stone was also incorporated in a naturalistic effect. No motorized equipment was used—just skilled labor with strong backs and willing arms, using old-fashioned tools.

Most of this original planting, particularly the shrubs surrounding the house, is still effective, though grown considerably larger. Most prominent are Sargent's hemlock (*Tsuga canadensis* 'Pendula'), Japanese hemlock (*T. sieboldii*), Japanese variegated maples (*Acer palmatum* 'Variegatum'), Japanese dwarf azaleas (*Rhododendron kiusianum*), *Kalmia latifolia* var. 'Ostbo Red', epimediums, and other ground covers. This first phase extended into the early war years, when progress was very slow because of the dearth of labor.

The second half acre, west of the house, presented some new problems, also tackled during the 1940s. This area was primarily a low, boggy depression; we installed a drainage system, filled the depression with many loads of soil, and then graded it. In 1949 a young

Anemonella thalictroides, the rue anemone, is a dainty woodland plant. Native to the eastern United States, it produces flowers that are usually single white or light pink, but it occasionally drifts west, and a unique double-pink form—an easy, long-blooming gem—was found in Minnesota and christened 'Schoaf's Double Pink'.

The gray-shingled house is sited on a rocky ridge commanding an ideal vista of the entire garden at all seasons. The bloom is greatest between March and July, with a green shade dominant throughout the year. Tall hundred-year-old oaks form the skeleton of the garden.

The large collection of rhododendrons and azaleas includes the extraordinary *Rhododendron macrosepalum* 'Linearifolium' from Japan. This unusual, decorative, and very distinctive azalea has long narrow leaves and lobes of the same shape, which are bright rose-lilac and hairy at the base.

Substantial native granite steps lead from the side driveway toward the front entrance of the house. Pockets along them contain such plants as *Trillium nivale* and, below that, *Epimedium* x *youngianum* 'Niveum', planted about fifty years ago and never lifted or divided—a testimonial to the longevity of a herbaceous plant. Note the oak on the right, with its dense cover of climbing *Hydrangea petiolaris*.

seedling of dawn redwood (*Metasequoia glyptostroboides*), discovered in western China in 1941, was planted in the lowest moist area. It is now at least ninety feet high and five feet in diameter at the base. Since the surrounding lawn would not extend to the base of the tree, a collection of shade plants creates a perfect planted oval.

In the same section are two large oaks with *Hydrangea petiolaris* 'Skyland Queen' planted at their bases. Now forty years old, these climbing hydrangeas are an awesome sight when in bloom, in May and June, extending their growth completely around the massive trunks to about seventy-five feet in height. Flowering immediately afterward, the closely related species *Schizophragma hydrangeoides* has as its host a neighboring oak. Other planted islands have groups of Japanese deciduous species rhododendrons in the Schlippenbachii subseries—*RR. weyrichii, quinquefolium, reticulatum, sanctum*, and others. Also represented are *Enkianthus campanulatus, E.c. albiflorus*, and *E. perulatus*, plus *Hydrangea serrata, H. involucrata*, and its double-flower form *H.i.* 'Hortensis'. Underplanted are epimedium, cimicifuga, arisaema, and some eastern American natives.

Immediately after the war we started to develop the last half acre. Our primary effort was the clearing of fifteen old oaks to create open areas and to provide more light. Other minor trees and shrubs were also removed, as were their roots. This operation, which took one skilled forester the major part of a winter, uncovered extensive stone ledges and outcrops that interfered with our plans both for screening neighboring houses and for other planting. We had to depend upon blasting to remove the excess stone, and this yielded sufficient material for the construction of boundary walls five feet high and several hundred feet long, as well as the foundation and base for a new greenhouse.

Some major large stones were positioned to produce varying elevations, and we then completed the planting of necessary screening trees—Carolina hemlocks (*Tsuga caroliniana*), magnolias, Japanese dogwood (*Cornus kousa*), *Rhododendron fortunei, Mahonia japonica, Corylopsis pauciflora* and *C. sinensis, Enkianthus perulatus*, and *Chamaecyparis obtusa*, underplanted with many ground covers. Other smaller trees and shrubs were interspersed among the retained oaks and dogwoods, and groups of azaleas were placed directly upon the rock surface of large, flat ledges and were then sufficiently covered with a mixture of soil and peat moss.

During the third phase, in 1948, when we expanded the dining room and added a family room and greenhouse, a flagstone dining terrace was also constructed. We have ensured our privacy here through the skillful selection and location of shrubs to supplement two existing oaks. Locust logs created a series of steps in a grass path leading from the terrace to open lawns. The shrubs planted among adjacent rock outcrops include *Buxus microphylla* 'Kingsville Dwarf', *Azalea indicum* 'Balsaminaflorum', and *Rhododendron kiusianum* 'Album', with a group of *Tsuga canadensis* 'Cole' as ground cover, dominated by a forty-year-old pendulous specimen of the same species, trained eight feet upright.

We have kept the moss-covered shaded woodland paths as originally conceived, with borders of ground covers among the trees and shrubs so that little of the soil is bare. In fact, the original landscape design of the garden has been respected, even with the continual introduction of new plant varieties—the borders have simply been increased and some of the lawn area has been reduced to accommodate them.

This woodland garden is still dominated by the old oaks, permitting light and air to filter through, particularly after the removal of lower limbs. But over the years the spreading canopy has lessened the penetration of sunlight, and now no area receives more than a couple of hours of direct sun daily. Naturally there is abundant sunlight throughout the

The dense border of *Hakonechloa macra* 'Aureola' is a yellow-striped form with slow-spreading twelve-inch leaves. In Japan it is usually grown in large low pots for its display of autumn color. Planted here under a tall *Pieris japonica* 'Contorta', it does not achieve the glorious red shades it assumes when exposed to full sunlight.

One of the glories of the eastern woodlands is the single bloodroot, a member of the poppy family. But its full double form, *Sanguinaria canadensis* 'Multiplex', is far superior—its stamens have been transformed into additional petals and produce beautiful round white globes that last much longer than the blossoms of the single form.

PLANT COLLECTORS

spring months, before the leaves emerge, and during this period carpets of small bulbs predominate, among them chionodoxa, scilla, fritillaria, galanthus, erythronium, narcissus, and other minor bulbs.

For many years the principal summer chore consisted of providing the plantings with enough irrigation. The soil, which is light and almost too well drained, needs to be watered periodically. The nuisance of hand-watering with hoses dictated a more efficient substitute, so about twenty years ago we installed an underground irrigation system. Almost all of the garden was covered in eight zones, with revolving sprinkler heads elevated about fifteen to twenty-five feet in strategic positions on the trunks of the oaks, with only a few on the ground to cover lawn areas. As a labor-saving device it was a most worthy investment.

Fortunately our home is at the heart of the property, so that we have views from three sides into a green garden, picturesque even in winter. A knowledgeable visitor will quickly discern that the plants in the garden are primarily from Japan (no less than 75 percent of the total) and the eastern United States. Our comparative success with plants from these two geographical areas has encouraged us to broaden the search for additional accessions. Consequently my wife and I have traveled throughout the world. While most of the areas we visited were fascinating, we found that hardy plants applicable to our climate were mainly found in Japan, Great Britain, and parts of Europe. We returned with many treasures—new and exotic flora, many of them first-time introductions here.

These horticultural exposures led me to concentrate on a few genera with a limited number of species and cultivars. The first effort was with epimediums. We planted a group of these enduring plants along some stone steps over fifty years ago, and they have not been disturbed since but have merely spread themselves discreetly within the area. Many species and hybrids have become the dominant underplanting throughout the garden.

Another genus of interest is tricyrtis, blooming from June to October with varying habit and flowers. The outstanding showy species cultivated here is *Tricyrtis macrantha*, which is planted on a huge rock outcrop in a rather shallow pocket in partial shade. It has prospered, producing long, trailing stems down the rock face and bearing its lovely tubular yellow flowers in the leaf axils in the autumn. Several other upright species grow in front of a group of taller azaleas among a bedding of dainty *Epimedium* x *youngianum* 'Niveum'.

A favorite primula from Japan is the long-cultivated *Primula sieboldii*. Perhaps the easiest for this garden, it has been established here in partial shade for many years, increasing and self-sowing in many places. Its flowers are extremely diversified in color, shape, and habit, and the plant itself has a defense mechanism that permits it to go dormant in the heat of the summer and then to reappear in the early spring if kept fairly moist. Planted amongst the primulas are ferns, arisaema, *Lilium canadense*, and other shade plants. Behind these is an impressive group of *Glaucidium palmatum*, in both the normal blue-lavender and the albino forms, and next to it are some four-foot *Kirengeshoma palmata*, blooming in late summer with pendulous lilylike yellow flowers.

Among the woody shrubs are attractive members of the enkianthus genus, mostly deciduous, spring-blooming, and of upright form. *Enkianthus perulatus*, which for unaccountable reasons is rather rare in this country, is perhaps the most popular small shrub in Japanese gardens. There it is used as a hedge of varying heights from one to six feet, but more often it is sheared into globular form, a practice that sacrifices the charming white flowers in spring in order to obtain the brilliant autumn color it produces when exposed to the sun. Planted in various areas of the garden are other species and forms of

The ground cover and foreground plantings predominating throughout the garden are epimedium species and their hybrids. The most eye-catching in flower is this *Epimedium grandiflorum* 'Rose Queen', a native of Japan. Though extremely hardy and adaptable to a variety of soils and conditions, this is one of the most underused families.

The plant that has evoked the most comment and consumed the largest quantities of color film here for the past twenty-five years is one of the Japanese jacks-in-the-pulpit, *Arisaema sikokianum*. A group of these are planted in a large bed of *Primula sieboldii* in damp partial shade.

enkianthus; the rarest is the dwarf compact form of *E. perulatus*, which measures less than two feet in height and diameter and is now over forty years old.

The rhododendron family is divided into various series with similar height and form. In the Series Azalea is the Subseries Schlippenbachii, which consists of about twelve species; most are represented here, as well as some of the albino forms, adding interest and beauty with their spring flowers and autumn foliage.

While this garden was developed by a keen plantsman, it would be remiss not to acknowledge the two women who have enjoyed major roles in its construction and maintenance. First, my wife, Esta, gave constant and wholehearted support and encouraged my dedication to the garden and to travel; and second, the British-trained horticulturist Lois Beckett Himes has provided faithful assistance over almost twenty-five years in the development and maintenance of all aspects of the garden.

John Gaston Fairey

Rhododendron austrinum, an outstanding selection from a lost source in Alabama, carries a mass of large flowers glowing cadmium-yellow in early April.

MY GARDEN IS at all times a magical place. It is an environment I have built for myself in a creative process that has become for me the most essential art form. It soothes and at the same time stimulates; feeling, smelling, hearing and tasting all come into play. To make a garden, one must be a dreamer, but a dreamer with fortitude, training one's mind to think of a myriad of things at once. The garden designer cannot consider texture, color, and rhythm today and tomorrow be concerned with function. There is no formula, and this is often frustrating, even for the most experienced gardener. It is not the garden but the act of creation that is the driving force.

To refresh my memories of magical times and places, I often return in thought to my youth in rural central South Carolina. As clearly as if it were yesterday, I remember the day I waded down a clear, spring-fed stream, following its meandering course into the deep and mysterious woods. Suddenly above and surrounding me was a *Stewartia malacodendron* in full bloom. This moment has had a lifelong effect on me. It opened my eyes to the beauty we too often overlook.

One hot and steamy July day in 1971, I took my first look at the seven acres that would become my garden. I walked away uninterested. Later that week, against my wishes, I was persuaded to take a second look. This time I made my way past the dilapidated house, chicken coops, and cow barn, forged through the jungle of native grapes, honeysuckle, and trumpet vines that was smothering the giant old trees, and pushed on into an opening that revealed a clear, spring-fed stream. It was the property I had been searching for, and what began innocently, as a pursuit of a sense of place, fast evolved into a passion.

The constant source of water that almost divides the property in half has had a tremendous impact on its development. I discovered that the quiet, bubbling water could be transformed into a raging torrent, and that heavy local rains—sometimes up to five inches in a short period—could raise the level of the creek by three or four feet. Although I was gardening on a mature woodland site, I experimented with native plants for flood and erosion control, channeling summer breezes, blocking winter winds, and reducing various visual and noise pollutants. One of my first tasks was to stabilize the banks by planting vast numbers of taxodium, betula, and nyssa. Today these trees are reaching forty feet and have been underplanted with many species of magnolia, acer, lindera, carpinus, cornus, and aesculus.

On May 20, 1983, a devastating tornado ravaged the garden. This disaster would forever change the direction of my thoughts. With the high canopy of mature trees gone, the magical light disappeared. It took the next five years to remove the damaged

Young cypresses, *Taxodium distichum*, frame a view across the stone bridge. The open expanse of lawn is bordered by a woodland setting dappled in mid-March with early-spring-flowering Indica azaleas and redbud.

This intimate spot was spared the brunt of the tornado of 1983. The heavy spring fogs are most beneficial to the camellias growing in this protected environment. *Camellia* 'South Seas' is one of the few hybrids that can withstand our abrupt changes of temperature.

trees and to rearrange the several understories. The woodland plants that had been nurtured by the dappled shade of these ancient trees were abruptly exposed to the searing Texas sun; fortunately the young trees planted during the early 1970s were flexible and were not affected by the treacherous winds. These *Acer saccharum* and *A. rubrum* var. *drummondii, Pinus glabra, P. elliottii, Carya ovata, Magnolia virginiana, Quercus texana*, and *Q. shumardii* are now developing new canopies and defining space. Some of them are even exposing a weaving of roots, giving the garden floor a new texture and character.

Although the tornado was disheartening, today I can only think of the positive new directions that have resulted from this fluke of nature. It gave me the opportunity to create a garden that better reflected my thoughts about space, and to investigate and experiment with new plants. For the first time I felt free to be in control of the design. I was able to envisage the garden as a series of exterior rooms, constructed with a wide variety of plants forming abstract versions of divides, walls, windows, doors, ceilings, and floors.

The question of how one moved through the garden became a major consideration. I have constructed a network of paths inviting visitors to meander, pause, stop, view the individual plant, reflect whence they have come, and anticipate the next turn. The series of intimate spaces within the garden is linked so that the journey seems to have neither a beginning nor an ending. Distances are deceptive. A sense of interior space is suggested

The complex layering of native and exotic trees and shrubs plays an integral part in the overall design of the garden.

by the canopy of single and grouped trees, by shrubs, and often by steps. A vast variety of plants, colors, and textures comes into play, but the garden as a whole is a balanced composition in which each element plays an equal role.

The spatial sequence is frequently given a sense of continuity by the rhythmic undulations of paths, grassy areas, and the two plants that I use most: clipped *Ilex vomitoria* and *Rhododendron macranthum* (*R. indicum*). My inspiration for the ilex, our native yaupon, came from the unique sculptural specimens found in local pastures. Years of cattle browsing the new growth have transformed these shrubs into miniature mountains, hills, and valleys of green. In addition, the female yaupon produces a glossy red berry that is attractive to the many kinds of birds that live here. And I use the macrantha azalea because this ancient Japanese satsuki forms a mass of dark-green foliage that shimmers in the light in all seasons. It retains this density even in winter and spot-blooms small, simple, salmon-orange flowers in May and June and again in October and November.

After the tornado I hired several assistants to help remove the fallen and damaged trees. I am indebted to John Talley, an ex-student, and to Carl Schoenfeld for their sincere interest and involvement in this tedious task. Their ingenious approach to removing broken limbs that were hanging precariously fifty to sixty feet above rare and prized shrubs was amazing. What began as a part-time job for Carl eventually evolved into a business partnership. His enthusiasm and natural feel for plants led him to investigate and advise on possible replacements for lost trees and shrubs, and as a result of his research untold numbers of rare and unusual plants have been introduced into the garden. Those varieties native to Texas and Mexico are still of primary interest, but many of their Asian counterparts are also now at home here.

Over the past several years I have taken part in numerous plant explorations into the mountains of northern Mexico. There is an overwhelming diversity of plants in this vast and ruggedly beautiful place, but overgrazing and other economic pressures are fast depleting many species. Usually accompanied by a botanist to help with problems of identification, I have collected over three hundred species of seed for testing in the garden.

A sunny area of the south perennial garden is alive with early-summer color. The outstanding red daylily 'Valentine's Day' is repeat-flowering and holds its color even in our extreme heat.

PLANT COLLECTORS

The undulating line of the grass invites the visitor into the west garden. The recently planted Satsuki azalea 'Chinsoy' will mass to emphasize the flow.

After several years of collecting, germinating, and growing these seeds, I have begun to develop a "dry" garden on the north side of the stream. This new area is quickly becoming an exciting addition to the garden.

Now, with a collection of over three thousand species and cultivars, I have begun to think of the garden not only as a continuing form of art in progress but also as a resource that must be used and shared. To this end, in 1988 Carl and I created a partnership in the mail-order Yucca Do Nursery at Peckerwood Garden so that we could share our plants with many other gardeners. The profits from the nursery business will keep the garden alive and growing and thus give me some assurance that this resource will not be lost.

The evolutionary process that has produced the garden as it exists today mirrors my own vision, but is also very much a synthesis, a collaboration. I am indebted to my family, with its long gardening tradition, and to Lynn Lowrey, who not only introduced me to my first Texas native plant but has also for twenty years continued to lend his support and knowledge. We who have worked here have shared a vision of the garden as process of change. As an artist, I have found in the garden a creative center for my design-research activity—a place where the artificiality of disciplinary boundaries has been exposed. It is a magical place indeed.

Robert Wm Grimes

MOUNT WASHINGTON,
LOS ANGELES, CALIFORNIA

I LIVE IN ONE of the relic woodsy areas near downtown Los Angeles. My garden is just under an acre in size, and it sprawls over a steepish, south-facing canyonside bounded by a street below, a street above, a neighbor to one side, and the pale of a vacant lot to the other. The garden, whimsically named Kissinghurst by a wandering poet, has never had an overall plan but instead has always represented my current "state of mind," in the broadest sense of that cliché.

My small redwood-sided cottage perches halfway up the slope, and when I bought the place about thirty years ago my first impression was of a flight of concrete steps joining front curb with front porch like some sort of stopped escalator. Awful. I soon corrected this by regrading to allow a meandering path.

Construction of the street above me many years ago resulted in a talus of shale rubble, which I subsequently inherited bound by a turf of wild barley roots. So, starting with that, I have gradually created proper soil by composting every scrap of anything biodegradable. (My compost heaps consist of whatever will decompose *plus* sand, bought locally by the sack, *plus* horse manure and straw, freely available from a nearby stable, *plus* some water now and then, *plus* lots of time.) I have also spread a foot or so of so-called mushroom mulch over the entire garden from time to time. This is the self-limiting medium that will not support more than three crops of mushrooms, if I am remembering correctly. It is a godsend and does not cost much.

I have stabilized the slope by creating naturalistic dry stone walls using the Arroyo Seco cobbles at hand, as well as by planting a wide variety of perennials accustomed to the hard life.

To the rear and to one side of the house I created a "Wollmanized" wood deck (the effective suggestion of a friend, the garden designer Chris Rosmini). The deck was built round an old California walnut tree, but I eliminated this venerable object after several years of messy menace from the falling walnuts.

The garden is divided into sectors. The front garden runs to blue and purple, with a mature *Duranta repens*, salvias, lavandulas, stokesias, larkspurs, and thistles as well as penstemons, hollyhocks, and an ineradicable patch of *Alstroemeria pulchella*. An enormous *Aristolochia californica* takes a sixty-year-old oleander in its suffocating embrace each year, and a mystery aralia has reached thirty feet in ten years. There are invasive clumps of *Dianella tasmanica*, a grove of *Tabebuia chrysotricha* grown from seed, *Bauhinia variegata*, and a significant stand of timber bamboo.

The front porch entry is wreathed with *Tetrastigma voinieranum* (*Vitis voinierana*), which has nothing to do with a grape.

The main slopes have a variety of drought-tolerant plants, including the white Matilija

The view from a high vantage point in the rear garden shows gaillardia (foreground) at the base of *Beaucarnea recurvata*, with a persimmon, *Diospyros kaki* 'Fuyu', to the left.

Brick paths meander, ramped up, down, and around. Here stepped, the path is flanked by *Heteromeles arbutifolia* (our native toyon), festooned with *Parthenocissus tricuspidata* (at left) and *Ampelopsis brevipedunculata* 'Elegans' (at right). The latter has remarkably beautiful greenish-ivory to metallic-blue berries in late fall.

The view from the rear deck (of "Wollmanized" lumber) up into a steep hillside planting of such exotics as *Juniperus chinensis* 'Kaizuka' (*J.s. torulosa*, right), *Chorisia speciosa* (center), and *Beaucarnea recurvata* against a green background of native bracken and ubiquitous small-leaved ivy. Seedlings are more than tolerated.

poppy (*Romneya coulteri*), *Linaria dalmatica*, a delightful plant and all-time survivor, and two others that have naturalized: the corn cockle, *Agrostemma githago*, and a South African annual, *Ceratotheca triloba*. *Gnidia squarrosa* is an old favorite, as are *Phlomis italica* and *Otatea acuminata* (ah, but *is* it going to seed?). *Echium fastuosum* has long been naturalized with minimal care, but *E. pininana* still plays hard-to-get. The garden is defined at the top of the slope by a hideous thorny hedge consisting largely of agaves. *Brodiaea capitata* (*Dichelostemma pulchellum*) is a delight in spring.

I have created a significant scree in the dryest part of the garden, and I call that area the Kalahari. It supports manfreda, ocotillo (*Fouquieria splendens*), Mexican tulip poppy (*Hunnemannia fumariifolia*), *Puya alpestris*, prickly phlox (*Leptodactylon californicum*), an impressive collection of South African moraeas (doing only so-so), hawkweed (thank you, Chris), *Aster divaricatus*, jatropha, a plumeria, and my favorite of all, *Echium wildpretii*.

The Plaza del Buen Maestro is the poorly kept secret of where all these paths lead. Atlas tells time there by means of a sundial mounted atop his awful burden. Palo verde (*Parkinsonia aculeata*) weeps while *Cleome spinosa* 'True Rose Queen' flourishes, along with a near-black scabiosa and an assortment of perennials and annuals, in a bounding raised planter.

About a third of the garden falls into the Midsummer Night's Dream sector to the rear. Photographers generally consider this part impossible to photograph because it is green-on-green—"No depth," they say. The greenery consists of a spinney of mayten tree (*Maytenus boaria*), cotoneaster, viburnum, laurel, floss-silk tree (*Chorisia speciosa*), and *Juniperus chinensis* 'Kaizuka' (syn. *J.c. torulosa*), full of Boston ivy and with bracken everywhere. *Clerodendrum bungei* has struggled through a couple of winters; *Crambe cordifolia* vegetates with no hint of flower; *Melaleuca incana* provides an agreeable gray contrast. There is also a grape arbor, which Chris Rosmini has suggested should be made of copper plumbing pipes. A splendid idea. It is now covered with an unruly mass of Concord grape (*Vitis labrusca*).

My garden survives lack of guidance during my annual absence of about three or four months. I am always surprised how overgrown and romantic it all looks when I return. What is its secret? It seems to do without me much better than I do without it.

The Plaza del Buen Maestro, dominated by Atlas bearing his heavy burden, is framed by the arching branches of *Parkinsonia aculeata*, with Japanese blood grass at its base and rudbeckia and bauhinia seedlings in the foreground. In the background (center) is *Annona cherimola*, which through hand pollination we have coaxed to bear fruit, resembling miniature hand grenades.

OCCASIONALLY I AM ASKED to speak at local garden clubs, and I am inclined to begin my talk by saying, "If you can garden in Dallas, you can garden anywhere." I base this observation on personal experience, which began when I moved into my house, in the fall of 1974. The entire place was in a deplorable condition, and there was not even a trace of a garden. I gave little thought to repairing the inside but instead directed my efforts toward ridding the grounds of an assortment of prickly brambles and an overabundance of hackberry trees, *Celtis occidentalis*.

My next project was to lay out the basic design of the garden. It was then that I discovered that the soil, a black clay with shards of chalk running through it, was impossible to work with. We had had a particularly hot and dry summer, with daily temperatures hovering well above 100°, which had left the soil hard and patterned by cracks up to two inches wide and sixteen inches deep. In retrospect, I think that was preferable to the condition of the soil when it got wet and turned into what is locally referred to as "gumbo." Trying to dig wet gumbo is almost impossible, since it clings to the spade in much the same way library paste sticks to a wooden paddle; it also adheres to shoes, layer by layer, until they are at least six times their normal size and weight. Replacing the clay with sandy loam would be the best way to prepare such beds, but it is more economical to improve the existing soil by tilling in a small amount of sand and a large amount of organic matter, which is precisely what I did.

My garden is small—fifty feet square—and was originally quite flat. By planning my line of sight from corner to corner rather than from side to side, however, it was possible to have seventy-foot vistas, giving the appearance of a much larger garden. To add interest I raised the soil level by two feet in one corner and built steps up to a small elliptical lawn. I decided to use evergreens as the background; when I began planting them I found that nearly all the members of the cedar, chamaecyparis, juniper, and holly ranges will do quite well in the summer heat of Texas. I am particularly fond of mixing different shades of conifers and find them invaluable for adding color to the garden in winter. *Juniperus chinensis* 'Spartan' is a good basic dark-green and contrasts well with *J. scopulorum repens* 'Wichita Blue'; used sparingly, the golden Hinoki cypress, *Chamaecyparis obtusa* 'Crippsii', adds a bright touch. Since these conifers reach a height of fifteen feet or more, I planted smaller varieties at the base, including the shiny dark-green *C. obtusa* 'Nana Gracilis', the bright-yellow *C.o.* 'Nana Aurea', and the blue *C. pisifera* 'Boulevard'. I have also had great success with heaths, specifically *Erica carnea* 'Springwood White' and the pink form, *E.c.* 'Winter Beauty', both of which tolerate lime and grow well in full sun.

To add interest to otherwise level ground, this area was built up by hauling in soil. The yellow tulips encircling the small elliptical lawn are 'Mrs. John T. Scheepers', and those behind the stone bench are 'Burgundy Lace'. Both are late-blooming cottage types and always dependable.

Where beds remain wet due to poor drainage, impatiens and *Hosta ventricosa* will thrive even in the heat of full Texas sun. Here they frame an Italian limestone urn.

Conifers not only provide a background for the garden but also add color that is particularly appreciated during the winter months. Tall golden Hinoki cypress (*Chamaecyparis obtusa* 'Crippsii') contrasts with *Juniperus scopulorum* 'Wichita Blue'. These are underplanted with *Thuja orientalis*, *Picea glauca* 'Albertiana Conica', *Chamaecyparis obtusa* 'Nana Aurea', and *C.o.* 'Nana'.

Although our unrelenting summer heat is a big problem, we can grow a variety of annuals and perennials extremely well. I generally mass the annuals *Impatiens sultanii* and *Begonia semperflorens* in wet places where they will do well even in full sun. In drier areas I mix marigolds (*Tagetes patula*), periwinkles (*Vinca rosea*, now *Catharanthus roseus*), *Salvia splendens, Ageratum houstonianum*, and blue haze (*Evolvulus nuttallianus*). While annuals provide a quick carpet of color, it is to perennials that I really devote most of my time, though I must confess that in this climate many of them—such as delphiniums— must be treated as annuals, or at least as biennials. Outstanding performers include the lythrums, all varieties of *Coreopsis verticillata*, rudbeckias, *Campanula persicifolia*, and *Achillea ptarmica*.

In winter there are fewer flowers to choose from, so I generally mass plantings of seasonal color. Viola cultivars do exceedingly well from October through May; I am especially fond of the smaller-faced "crystal bowl" varieties. Since my house is partially constructed of a local rust-colored stone, I prefer to use the yellow or blue shades to outline borders. Behind the pansies I mix ornamental cabbage (*Brassica oleracea* 'Sikito') and ornamental kale in the white, pink, or purple shades. Stocks (*Matthiola incana*) lend their spicy fragrance all winter if temperatures stay above 28°, and it is possible to protect them even on those few nights when the temperature dips lower. It is then that I pile

In small areas a feeling of depth is important. Planning the garden from corner to corner, rather than from side to side, can lengthen the visual axes by 30 percent.

straw liberally on my more tender flowering plants, though as a rule it is necessary to leave them covered only for two or three days.

In semi-shade I use *Cyclamen persicum*; these will easily remain hardy down to 22° and even lower if they are covered. My standard flowering plants for light shade are primulas and polyanthus, which start to bloom in November and continue through to the end of April. I like to plant them in dense masses and am particularly fond of the bright blue, red, and yellow tones—the flowers look like jewels set in the shadier parts of the garden. Often I will dig and pot a plant to bring inside the house for a few days; the yellow ones seem to be the most fragrant and smell rather like freesias.

I suppose I appreciate my garden most during the cold months. Although most gardens are planned for summer, in our climate they are certainly more enjoyable in winter. Usually the days require only a sweater, weeds cease to be a problem, nature provides most of the watering, the heat of the summer is forgotten, the incessant Texan insects have gone dormant, and the conifers display their most brilliant hues of blue, green, purple, bronze, and yellow. In late afternoon the sun casts long shadows across the lawn, and the colors appear more intense than ever.

The housing for the building's elevator shaft is fitted with a shelf for terra-cotta pots of cleome and ageratum. The large wooden boxes hold *Thuja occidentalis* 'Spiralis' underplanted with draping *Rosa* 'The Fairy', cotoneaster, and *Phalaris arundinacea* 'Picta'.

The apartment is on two levels, each with a greenhouse. The building's water tower not only is the crowning focal point of this roofscape but also provides perfect spaces for hanging baskets of petunias, verbena, and lobelia above boxes containing *Rosa* 'Don Juan' and clematis. Beyond is the Central Park reservoir.

I HAD BEEN LIVING IN MY penthouse apartment on the West Side of Manhattan for six months before I saw the roof of the building. It was a slightly sloped tar surface furnished with every kind of mechanical equipment imaginable. In spite of this, the spectacular views — over the entire expanse of Central Park to the East Side and midtown, and westward to the Hudson River and the New Jersey Palisades — made the site irresistible. Besides, there was a very good feeling of space, and I decided to make my dream house and garden on this formidable roof.

Shortly after my discovery, I asked my friend and colleague the landscape architect Bruce Kelly to look at the roof with me. While cautioning me about the enormous effort that would be required to make the project work, he too recognized the potential of the space and encouraged me to go forward with my idea. He made the intriguing suggestion that I consider putting part of the area into lawn, since the roof was big enough to have a real garden feeling. That idea was zany enough to appeal to me, and from that moment I went forward with building a spectacular rooftop terrace garden.

The whole history would fill volumes. But to give an idea of the complications, I will point out that all the mechanical equipment had to be relocated without reducing its function; a railing had to be added to meet the housing code; and a hole had to be punched into the roof from my apartment below, though we had no idea of how thick the roof was—all this before I could even begin to plan my dream garden.

The terrace garden that evolved is L-shaped, with a new conservatory/dining room on top of the hole I had knocked through from below. The space overlooking Central Park is on an axis defined by the building's existing water tower. The tower, which had pretty good bones, needed to be restored—with new columns, repointing and replacement of the masonry, and coloring of the new bricks—before I could lattice the three arched openings on its second level. In front of the lattice I added three antique iron hanging baskets and, on the floor beneath the arches, three large wooden boxes. In these I planted roses, clematis, nepeta, petunias, lobelias, and a luxuriant display of verbena. My neighbors in the building to the south were particularly skeptical at the onset of my construction; now, however, they are quite appreciative of the way the renovations have improved their view.

The terrace on the Central Park side was then divided into two parts. Below the tower is the lawn, which has on each corner a huge square wooden box furnished with a fourteen-foot-tall arborvitae underplanted with buddleia, irises, grasses, and fairy roses, with cotoneaster draping over the sides of the box. On one side of the lawn I have created a composition of potted plants on a shelf against the elevator shaft, and on the other side are two formal points, outfitted with changing annuals and roses,

CITY AND TOWN

where clematis grows on the rail overlooking the park. The rest of the Central Park side of the terrace, and on around the corner, is raised up two steps and paved with bold parquet panel decking, designed to be removed in an emergency. It is on this corner, with its awe-inspiring views, that I live.

I have furnished the corner with a big tapestry-covered wicker sofa, four commodious wooden deck chairs, and, in the corner itself, my stargazing telescope. Along the rail I have arranged a symmetrical group of planters, including big blue ceramic pots each featuring a 'Betty Prior' rose and underplanted with nepeta, baby's breath, blue perennial salvias, and white petunias. Bruce Kelly says it looks like a wedding bouquet. In between the pots are wrought-iron Victorian plant stands tumbling with ivy and terra-cotta pots with globemaster arborvitae — that overused plant of the 1940s and '50s which takes on a new personality here and adds structure and winter color to the composition. In the corner I have planted a 'Don Juan' rose to give me a colorful summer filigree.

This sitting space also adjoins the part of the terrace away from the park, where the conservatory divides the park-view terrace from the river-view terrace. The large weeping willow next to the conservatory gives the entire terrace a wonderfully romantic feeling. The willow, the conservatory, and a small Katsura tree nestle my seating area as it faces into the wide blue yonder of Manhattan.

Conical thujas flanked by yellow-gold dahlias echo the verticality of Manhattan. The tight round shrubs along the rail are globemaster arborvitaes. *Miscanthus sinensis* 'Gracillimus' grasses stand in pots on the steps.

An airy, delicate composition of *Nepeta mussinii*, gypsophila, white petunias, and the 'Betty Prior' rose grows in a big blue urn against a railing overlooking Central Park.

A wrought-iron Spanish wellhead in the center of the river-view lawn serves as a place for hanging baskets. Each corner has a pagoda tree underplanted with annuals, perennials, and ground cover. The trees will grow together to form a gateway.

The sundial is centered on a narrow passage alongside the conservatory. It is edged by a shelf holding pots of dusty miller combined with lobelia between boxes of gomphrenas.

Next to the conservatory, in the narrow passage that divides the two terrace areas, I built a solid parapet with a double shelf. Here rows of planters are filled with annuals — gomphrenas, snapdragons, lobelias, and artemesia — to enliven the smallest room of my garden.

The back, or river-view, terrace overlooks the terrace and greenhouse adjoining my apartment on the floor below. (This lower terrace is part of the original architecture of the building; the greenhouse is new and aligned with the upper conservatory.) The river-view terrace is also divided into distinct spaces. The first, a continuation of the deck, contains a sundial and a large lead demilune planter filled with salvias. The next space, down two steps from the deck, is lawn, defined by four great wooden planters with four matching Japanese pagoda trees (*Sophora japonica*). Under these I have planted matching compositions of euonymus, hosta, ferns, and wisteria, all tolerant of the shade that I anticipate from the sophoras as they grow. For this part of the terrace I designed a simpler version of the antique railing that I purchased in England and used on the Central Park side. Opposite the railing, a warm flesh-pink stucco wall masks the ugly residual roof machinery. Beyond the lawn and up two steps again is the third space, the one closest to the Hudson River — a wooden deck area distinguished by a large planter that frames my narrow view of the river. Here I have used purple-leaved plum and autumn olive to give the edge of the terrace an abundant, overgrown feeling. An existing brick wall is planted with climbing hydrangea.

At the time of writing, my terrace garden is not yet six months old, but already it has shown me how it will develop in richness and interest — reward indeed for all the difficulties of establishing a container garden on what used to be a derelict rooftop in Manhattan.

George Radford

BANKVIEW
VICTORIA, BRITISH COLUMBIA

IN 1983 WE DECIDED TO JOIN other friends who were restoring Victorian and Edwardian properties in Victoria West. Ours is a large, picturesque corner house that sits on a steeply sloping hillside overlooking the Gorge Waters, north of Victoria's famous Inner Harbour, on Vancouver Island.

"Bankview" was buried in weeds, blackberries, and great swathes of morning glory, and the modest garden area was surrounded by an overgrown hedge of *Chamaecyparis lawsoniana*. The wide veranda around the house and its elaborate railings and columns were totally enveloped by the same trees—thirty feet high and half dead. However, a few specimen shrubs survived in the tangle.

We agreed that the first year would be spent restoring the house—then we would move on to the garden. When we removed the trees around the veranda, we uncovered at the base of each column a large gnarled root, with two rose briers growing from one of them. We packed rich compost around this survivor and watered it regularly with phostrogen.

The house, built in 1893, has all the characteristically angular lines of the Queen Anne style of architecture popular at the time. We thought it best to continue these lines when designing the planting layout. In order to have the maximum space for plants, our first major decision was: no lawns.

In volume 3 of our treasured set of Avray Tipping's *Gardens Old and New* we had always loved the pictures of Goddards, and we finally chose this terraced design, using rock walls, stairways, columns, and a pool on the lowest level in an adaptation of that delightful Lutyens and Jekyll garden. Only darker, weathered rock was used, so that the plants appeared to be displayed on an old stone foundation—not unlike parts of Vita Sackville-West's garden at Sissinghurst. In winter, when plants are not spilling in such profusion over the rock walls or the gravel paths, the strong but pleasant lines of the design are clearly visible—a unity of house and garden.

In April 1985 the rock construction was completed and the clay soil enriched with well-rotted leaves and mushroom and chicken manure. A passion for plants was paramount in our planning: while we desired to have a fair amount of year-round color and material to admire and cut, our ambition was to form a collection of the plants we loved without its looking like a collection!

Planting began with a large collection taken from our previous garden, including mature hostas, ferns, hardy geraniums, perennials, and shrubs. As founding members of the Victoria Horticultural Society's hardy-plant study group, we were also showered with choice plants. These had to be placed carefully to allow the different textures, lines, color shadings, and leaf shapes to interweave and create a panoramic collage—

Pink *Saponaria ocymoides* ramps over the gravel and around the silver feathers of *Artemisia* 'Powis Castle'. *Aucuba japonica* 'Variegata', thriving under the holly tree, will provide foliage for winter decoration.

The four-year-old circle of *Stachys byzantina*, lavender, and *Santolina chamaecyparissus*, nearly complete, gives a Victorian touch to this dry area. The rosettes of rose-pink *Geranium palmatum* can survive a mild winter; seedlings pop up in the gravel and make splendid foliage plants in large urns.

The drooping Norway spruce, *Picea abies* 'Inversa', cascades over a wall under the jutting prow of our house, located on a steep hill. Astrantias, hostas, and rodgersias thrive in a thick mulch of rotted mushroom manure, and silvery *Helichrysum petiolare* sends forth sprays from the Chinese urn.

especially when viewed from the veranda above, where many an evening has been spent either entertaining or working out our next step.

Now, when we lift the latch of the front picket gate on a hot summer's day, lavender perfumes the air from the round bed on the left, and the surrounding low hedge of *Santolina chamaecyparissus* releases its pungent scent. A wide border of lamb's ears, *Stachys byzantina*, spreads over the gravel, seeming to pick up a touch of pink from the *Geranium endressii* massed on the low wall. *Campanula portenschlagiana* is weaving its blue bells below and through the geranium, and above these three, *G. palmatum* makes exotic rosettes of large leaves and tall orchidlike flower stems.

Straight ahead, an iron arch is enveloped by a white-flowered *Clematis montana*— arch and clematis both moved from an old garden—and to one side, a standard *Wisteria sinensis* has its roots sheltered by *Geranium oxonianum* 'Claridge Druce', into which *Helichrysum petiolare* 'Limelight' is threading its filigree branches.

As we descend the first flight of steps, the statue of Flora, shaded by a group of old

The pool area has a bold planting that includes the umbrella-like leaves of *Petasites japonicus* and the massive heads of *Euphorbia characias wulfenii*. *Hedera helix* 'Goldheart' spreads over the pool edges, and variegated *Lunaria annua* lights up a corner.

holly trees, beckons us from a distance. Blue *Viola cornuta* ramps around the base of the steps and into clumps of hostas, *Hosta lancifolia* and *Smilacina racemosa*, shaded by a small halesia (Carolina tree). An edging of *Polygonum affine* 'Dimity' is spreading its hot-pink flower spikes over the gravel. On the left, masses of *Astrantia major*, *A.m.* 'Sunningdale Variegated', and white *Geranium sylvaticum* surround a Chinese urn filled with silvery-gray *Helichrysum petiolare* and pink pelargoniums. *Alchemilla mollis* and a large *Salvia officinalis* 'Purpurascens' spill over the edge of the wall.

The branches of *Flora*'s sheltering holly canopy start about seven feet from the ground. In this part of the garden is a lovely combination of Bowles' golden grass (*Milium effusum* 'Aureum'), *Geranium endressi*, and *Corydalis lutea*. For richer contrast there is a collection of ferns, oxalis, and miniature hostas growing in profusion, backed by the spiky, shining green leaves of *Iris foetidissima*. On the boundary trellis, a blue-flowered *Clematis macropetala* is reaching up into the hollies.

Down the second flight of stairs, a wide gravel path reaches into the distance, edged with spreading thymes, gold origanum, dianthus, *Campanula carpatica*, saxifrages, and mounds of pink and white armeria. Terminating the vista is a small statue on a column, surrounded by groups of hostas and *Pulmonaria officinalis* 'Sissinghurst White', *P.* 'Rubra', and *P.* 'Mrs. Moon'. An edging of red-flowered *Mimulus cardinalis* expands into the gravel below.

Hydrangea quercifolia leans over the steps, and *H. macrophylla*, deliciously dotted with clusters of foamy pink flowers, are shaded by the hollies. The finely divided leaves of a tree peony remind us of its silky white flowers and of the friend who raised it from seed. A tall planting of bronze fennel waves its slender stems in the wind, with masses of brilliant white *Corydalis alba* and sweet-scented, yellow-belled hemerocallis mingling at its base. Nearby, violet sweet rocket (*Hesperis matronalis*) perfumes the evening air.

The pool reflects the bay window directly above it, as well as the ever-changing sky. Clumps of white callas (*Zantedeschia aethiopica*), *Iris pseudacorus*, *Filipendula palmata*, *Hosta sieboldiana* 'Elegans', ferns, and *Petasites japonicus* edge the water, while a planting of *Scirpus lacustris tabernaemontani* grows beside the cherubs of the fountain, and *Hedera helix* 'Goldheart' spreads along the rim of the pool. This area is regularly visited by a family of racoons, so we have no fish.

In the far corner towers a splendid old *Taxus baccata*, a majestic dark-green presence. Its long branches seem to wave to us as we garden. In front of it we planted *Viburnum* x *bodnantense* 'Dawn' for winter flowers and a group of *Artemisia lactiflora* for the feathery white plumes in summer.

Our mature hostas have settled in well. The pride of the place is *Hosta plantaginea* 'Grandiflora', along with *H. sieboldii* and *H. fortunei* 'Aureo-marginata'. From the trellis, *Clematis montana* 'Tetrarose' has sent up a few vines into the yew.

A small plant of *Euphorbia characias wulfenii*, given us by a special friend, was soon happy nearby, growing rapidly and creating a focal point—such a wonderful contrast to the other foliage, and a joy in winter when the hostas are sleeping. *Dicentra spectabilis* thrives in the rich soil, and we enjoy its delightful pink lockets before the hosta leaves unfurl and dominate. *Anemone* x *hybrida*, in shades of pink, rose, and white, reward us for a long while after the flowers have faded with their elegant shiny foliage and their glaucous seedheads. The celadon-shaded leaves and starry-white flower spikes of *Lysimachia ephemerum* have proved to be an interesting contrast.

As we turn at the back of the house, the silver clouds of *Artemisia* 'Powis Castle' glow in the sunlight—a reminder of another friend who carried a cutting from England.

In front of this is *Geranium sanguineum*, a form with rich claret flowers. The artemisia has grown gradually and blended with a nearby blue *G. wallichianum* 'Buxton's Variety'.

As we ascend the steps, *Rheum palmatum* 'Atrosanguineum' rises over us in a fountain of burgundy. *Gentiana asclepiadea* hangs its blue flowers over the wall above the pale-yellow *Phygelius aequalis* 'Yellow Trumpet'. The background of this higher planting contains silver *Onopordum acanthium*—a perfect foil for *Geranium psilostemon*, white phlox, and *Centaurea macrocephala*. The foreground mixture of miniature hostas, 'Jackman's Blue' rue, and *Coreopsis verticillata* is softened by trails of variegated vinca.

In spring, a small-flowered philadelphus radiates its perfume for weeks near the back door. *Lonicera etrusca* has twisted its way up into the gnarled remnant of a cherry tree, which also provides shelter for a prized housewarming gift, the azalea *Rhododendron schlippenbachii*. Many bulbs, large and small, are multiplying. Primroses, forget-me-nots, foxgloves, and wallflowers all have their corners. The rose by the veranda column grew vigorously, sending up new briers that flowered! It turned out to be Dean Hole's favorite—'Gloire de Dijon'.

Today, as we continue to seek out special plants for our horticultural tapestry, we are still often reminded that no garden, regardless of size, is ever completely finished.

The white spathes of *Zantedeschia aethiopica* rise from their soggy home above the lush summer foliage. A seedling plant of *Geranium palmatum* has spread its flowers over the petasites leaves. Double feverfew (*Tanacetum parthenium*) and *Astrantia major* 'Shaggy' light up the shady background.

THE GARDEN OF

Craig Bergmann and
James Grigsby

WILMETTE, ILLINOIS

IT WAS MY BIRTHDAY, and my father gave me a present—a very special present for a five-year-old, but one that has since shaped my life. This gift was a 20′ x 20′ garden, edged in stone, tilled, and ready for planting. It was hard to believe it was just for me. With his guidance I set to work immediately, laying brick paths and shopping for plants. I tended to my garden happily all through grammar school. Twenty-five years later, as I meditate on my present garden, fond memories of that little plot naturally intrude.

Ours is a city garden, a young garden. There are three buildings on our property, determining five gardening spaces. The largest of these spaces is completely enclosed and contains the major collection of plants. I remember sitting in this area six years ago with my partner, James Grigsby, when we asked ourselves, "What does this room need?"

The room was not entirely empty. Sheltered at one end, a forty-year-old *Magnolia* x *soulangeana* gave graceful shade to our turn-of-the-century greenhouse, a castoff from a nearby high school. Magnolias of this size are uncommon here, as they are liable to be destroyed by ice storms. Long before we arrived, this tree was the pride of the neighborhood. Obviously it had to stay, and would provide the canopy necessary for our shade garden.

The remainder of the large room consisted of four walls, a concrete walk along the side of the house, and a lawn. We learned that these walls were a double-edged sword— they could provide a beautiful backdrop for the garden, but they also inhibited the amount of sunlight the plants would receive. Over the years a good deal of experimentation was required to discover which plants would thrive here.

At the same time we set to work covering the walls themselves: one with trumpet vine (*Campsis radicans*), Boston ivy (*Parthenocissus tricuspidata*), sweet autumn clematis (*Clematis maximowicziana*), and the climbing rose 'Kathleen'; another wall with *Hydrangea petiolaris*; and the two-story house wall with a silver lace vine (*Polygonum aubertii*). Before long we had green walls for six months of the year—a wonderful backdrop. However, these plants truly know no bounds. They require frequent pruning and tend to rob the border of moisture.

The decision to remove the straight concrete walk and replace it with meandering bluestone not only softened the approach to the house but provided an additional planting area. We filled this with modern and antique roses and a specimen *Cornus mas* 'Golden Glory', all hedged with boxwood, lavender, and heuchera. The walk is now bordered by *Phlox divaricata*, sweet woodruff, a *Viburnum opulus* 'Compactum', a collection of ferns, and a drift of Virginia bluebells with Rembrandt tulips.

An edge of the silver gardens shows our interest in texture. The dwarf columbine *Aquilegia flabellata* 'Nana Alba' contrasts with the deep tones of *Heuchera micrantha* 'Palace Purple' and black parrot tulips.

Sleeping giants: five vines—*Parthenocissus tricuspidata, Hedera helix, Campsis radicans, Clematis indivisa* (*C. paniculata*), and *C. x jackmanii*—will soon come to life at the back of the long border.

Beyond the curving lawn, the approach to the patio is made inviting by *Iris pumila* hybrids, *Linum perenne* 'Blau Saphir', *Myosotis sylvatica* 'Victoria', and baskets of Imperial pansies. In summer the foliage of the eastern redbud, *Cercis canadensis*, shades the patio and the entry to the studio building.

Reducing the existing lawn by two thirds yielded a sunny perennial border forty-five feet long and eight feet deep. Many of our early plantings here were of woody materials, which added year-round texture and stature. Among our choices were the white fringe tree (*Chionanthus virginicus*), serviceberry (*Amelanchier canadensis*), *Hydrangea quercifolia*, and *Azalea* 'Herbert'. The scheme is multicolored and all of the flowers are perennial. The garden actually begins in April and blooms nonstop through October. This continuous show of color was our challenge.

As time went on, the lawn became smaller still, due to "tumblers" such as *Coreopsis* 'Moonbeam', *Aster* 'Professor Anton Kippenberg', and *Viola* 'Jersey Gem'. Antique granite paving brick from an old estate became a mowing strip to preserve what was left of a postage-stamp lawn. We learned the value of close-cropped turf—it provides a perfect foil for the garden, and the granite strip is like the fringe on a plush carpet.

The garden area nearest the bluestone patio seemed a perfect spot to indulge our interest in silver foliage. A 'Skyrocket' juniper with a dwarf blue spruce at its base provides the height, and *Iris pumila, Artemisia ludoviciana* 'Silver King', avena and blue fescue grasses, x *Pardancanda morrisii, Aquilegia flabellata* 'Nana Alba', *Sedum reflexum*, and woolly and silver thymes complete the grouping.

It is September as we write this, and we are sitting on the patio for a moment of rest. What we see gives us great pleasure: the 'Betty Prior' roses and the fountain grass are in full bloom at the kitchen door, the rich colors of the perennial asters, particularly the magenta of 'Andenken an Alma Pötschke', command attention, and from the top of the wall the fragrance of the sweet autumn clematis drifts our way. It is a moment to remind ourselves that this is still a young garden and to remember the words of the landscape artist Jens Jensen: "It will be interesting for you to note the changes that will take place as things now in youth grow into maturity. It is really first in maturity that life is most beautiful—when it has run its journey and speaks its story complete."

Early July brings the greatest variety to our garden. A profusion of pinks blend and contrast against the ivy-covered wall: *Lilium* 'Pink Tiger', *Malva alcea fastigiata*, *Astilbe* x *arendsii* 'Hyacinth', *Heuchera* x *brizoides* 'Coral Cloud', and the Polyantha rose 'The Fairy'.

Rosie recumbent in a garden room leading to the patio. In the foreground is a mix of hybrid lilies, a *Rhododendron mucronulatum*, and woodland strawberries; along the house are a *Cornus mas* 'Golden Glory' and the Floribunda rose 'Heirloom'; and at the patio edge are a dwarf blue spruce, *Lamium maculatum* 'White Nancy', avena grass, and *Iris pumila*.

Phillip Watson

WASHINGTON GARDENS
FREDERICKSBURG, VIRGINIA

MY GARDEN BEGAN six years ago as a blank page—no trees, no walkways, and no foundation plantings. Luckily there were old but operable greenhouses in which to produce much of the plant material I use; these were originally of raw cinderblock, which I proceeded to coat annually with a thick layer of lime mixed with water. That was the cheap part.

Tying the complex together was not so simple nor so cheap. I covered the roofs of the main house and the central greenhouse structure with cedar shakes to help unify the grounds and enclosed the entire back garden in solid fencing, not only to create a garden room but also to provide protection and privacy for my garden inhabitants, both human and animal. Then I latticed the side windows of the greenhouses to make them resemble garden structures that reflected more than utility. Where the pool is now, there was once an enormous iris bed. (As you know, an iris is a thing of beauty for only two weeks.) I did not want to eliminate the look of a garden in that central area, so I opted for a reflected garden—hence the black pool.

"Is it a pond or is it a pool?" was the question that made me realize that my endeavor had been successful. I think that one of the reasons the scheme works is the fact that the pool was designed to fit the garden, as opposed to the garden's being designed to fit the pool. The dark interior allows for a doubling effect in the garden and causes the small perennial border to seem more expansive. Borders of color spill almost into the pool, tipped by the white verbena, which looks like foam on the crest of a wave. Moonlit evenings are especially magical, when the scents of *Nicotiana sylvestris,* four o'clocks (*Mirabilis jalapa*), and moonflowers (*Ipomoea alba*) permeate the air. Daytime finds the garden alive with all sorts of birds; the mockingbirds, my favorite garden companions, are by far the most prevalent as well as the most audible. These sultans of summer especially enjoy the seeds on the lantana standards and by eating them allow the shrubs to bloom continuously. Although my densely planted borders afford little room for weeds, a recently enlarged family of brown rabbits has kept even the short weeds out. In June, while I was dead-heading the 'Joan Elliott' campanula, two young rabbits emerged from beneath a great clump of 'Moonshine' yarrow; now they are so tame they are almost like pets.

The borders that surround the pool achieve constant color through the use of perennials that are tall, narrow, and competitive. Just as the 'Starfire' phlox fades, the swamp

The fragrant flowering of *Nicotiana sylvestris* signals the arrival of the hummingbirds. Rising out of the mass is the finely dissected foliage of *Hibiscus coccineus*, which will hold court in August for the monarch butterflies.

A host of sun-loving perennials is reflected in the waters of the black pool, including silver artemisia, purple-leaved annual hibiscus, and orange *Zinnia angustifolia*. White flowers— *Cleome hasslerana* 'Helen Campbell', *Phlox paniculata* 'Mount Fuji', and (at far right) *Achillea ptarmica* 'Ballerina'—are reinforced by the white-painted birdhouse and latticed planter. The use of tall plants with small or narrow foliage permits dense planting, since little shade is produced and shorter plants can prosper beneath them.

Across an expanse of Blue Ridge flagstones, the Stone Mountain daisy, *Viguiera multiflora*, a flat-topped solidago, and *Helianthus giganteus* paint the September garden with golden hues. A touch of scarlet is added by the perennial *Hibiscus coccineus*.

A profusion of flowers gives a cottage-garden effect to the front yard. *Lythrum salicaria* 'Robert' has jumped the eyelet fence, leaving behind its taller *L.s.* ancestor. Brightening the spires of loosetrife are the six-inch spotlights of *Achillea* 'Moonshine'.

hibiscus rises above it, unfurling its enormous crimson blossoms. It is not long before hummingbirds and monarch butterflies blanket the border. By August the border is about to breach its banks of Japanese boxwood, and in spots *Zinnia angustifolia* spill over like molten lava. September finds the garden in a golden glow of Stone Mountain daisies, helenium, and the glorious twenty-foot-tall *Helianthus giganteus,* which was collected along the railroad tracks between Midnight and Panther Burn, Mississippi.

As the days become shorter and the twilight stretches longer, the hedge of *Chamae-cyparis obtusa* 'Crippsii' begins to catch that fleeting yellow light that comes just before sundown. It is a warming sight I take pleasure in the entire winter long. As frost overtakes the border and its perennials prepare for winter, the clipped forms once again stand out and assume leadership of the garden. Not only do I enjoy these evergreens for themselves, but I am also reminded that in July there was once a dazzling clump of crocosmia in front of the golden chamaecyparis cone, and that in September asters of royal purple stood alongside the fastigiate yew. These clipped forms prod the memory of a gardener who recalls wonderful things.

Jimmy Graham

I AM A FARMER. I grew up on a farm—not a plantation—in Union Springs, Alabama, and I cannot remember a time when I have not planted. My grandfather, a farmer in the same sense, was a great gardener. From him, and from the woods of Alabama, I learned much that I needed to know. Although it is difficult to pinpoint my approach to gardening, I will say that it is mostly an intuition, rooted in the past yet ever-changing, for the way I want things to look.

In my garden I have striven to create an American version of an English cottage garden. It is neatly maintained and at the same time overplanted. While I have not created a formal planting, the garden does achieve some measure of formality through its ornamentation, tended lawns, and separate rooms.

My wife, Mary Ann, and I moved to our eighty-year-old house ten years ago, shortly after our son, Kent, was born, and began work on the garden even before the previous owners had moved out. At the time the garden had what the English refer to as good bones: originally planted in the forties, it had some good trees, a fine but overgrown row of hollies, brick paths, and arches.

We spent the first six months clearing trees and cleaning up. During the next few years I erected walls and fences for privacy and a more secluded feeling. Rooms began to take shape, some out of necessity, others out of invention. In the back behind the open lawn, for example, we needed to gain access to an alley, and this need created the opportunity for a new spot with a totally different atmosphere. Here a brick and gravel path now meanders through dogwoods, lavenders, 'Judge Solomon' azaleas, hostas, and ferns, in sharp contrast to the sunny borders and manicured lawn just a few feet away. Heading in the opposite direction, this path also leads to the "secret garden," where 'Pride of Mobile' (syn. 'Elegans Superba') azaleas, pear trees, and leucothoë surround a patio area that seems miles from the busy street a few hundred feet beyond the fence.

Another area is the fish pool, added two years ago, in part out of a need for drainage, but also because I wanted to add an element of water to the garden. When the tiny pool was first constructed, I hated it—the concrete edges looked so stark and new. Since then, however, *Vinca minor* and moss have softened those hard edges, and Japanese iris, ornamental grasses, and cyperus have thrived around it. Wax myrtles flank the pool and its guardian gargoyle on either side. In the pool itself water lettuce, lilies, and papyrus flourish.

People often ask me about my theory on color. My only theory, I reply, is that I have no theory, but even this is not strictly true. As an interior designer, I strive for unusual color combinations. Every room must have an element of surprise—perhaps a touch of

Where sun meets shade, a teak chair designed by Charles Verey awaits the visitor. Pots of geraniums, hibiscus, ferns, and bougainvillea add different levels of color. Tulip magnolia and 'Judge Solomon' azaleas line the path. The jade plant is ten years old.

In front of the toolhouse Sweetheart roses and Lady Banks climbing roses soften the structure provided by carefully pruned English boxwood and dwarf yaupon hollies. *Clematis* 'Henryi', jasmine, wisteria, and red honeysuckle entangle the lattice fence surrounding this secret, cottage-style part of the garden.

Looking through the iron arbor and a frame of 'Blaze' roses, pyracantha, honeysuckle, silver-lace vine (*Fallopia baldschuanica* [syn. *Polygonum Aubertii*]), and Confederate jasmine (*Jasminum nitidum*). The brick path is lined with Victorian rope terra-cotta edging tiles. On the left stands a terra-cotta chimneypot, adding a clean, vertical dimension to the garden.

red or yellow in a room full of otherwise predictable combinations. That same delight in surprise also governs what I plant where in the garden. I do not particularly care about plant height, texture, or color so long as I achieve the effect I want.

As a result, the garden in back flaunts colors in the gaudiest manner. On the arches, yellow Lady Banks roses alternate with Carolina jasmine, purple and red honeysuckle, and other climbers, including red pyracantha and cotoneaster. This variety produces nearly continuous color and surprise throughout the growing season. Elsewhere, *Rudbeckia* 'Goldsturm', liatris, purple coneflower, lythrum, and all colors of phlox bloom during the hot summer months.

The plantings in the front of the house, on the other hand, though still unpredictable, are much more carefully planned for texture and color. Azaleas, hostas, astilbe, and daylilies appear in mauves, pinks, lavenders, and reds—not exactly what one might expect against the raspberry-sherbet exterior of the house. Interesting texture is provided by the *Ilex cornuta* 'Burfordii' pruned to resemble parasols, the precisely sheared boxwoods, and the less structured foliage of the azaleas, astilbe, and hostas.

While I do not have strict views of color and design, I do see certain needs and shortcomings in American gardens. Unlike the English, we have enormous spaces in which to garden, and these spaces are beautifully manicured. But our gardens lack an atmosphere of antiquity; they look too new, without that peaceful quality their English counterparts have of seeming to have been in existence forever. Of course we do not have the benefit of the wonderful old stone walls and ornaments that add so much character to English gardens; we can, however, furnish our American gardens with smaller old things. A bed of perennials is not complete until you have set something old in it—perhaps a terra-cotta pot overgrown with vines, or a statue, or a jardiniere.

In my own garden, my most prized possession is an eighteenth-century griffin that hovers over the fish pool. In another spot is a reproduction of the original jardiniere from Harewood House, Yorkshire. Benches and seats are everywhere, inviting the visitor to rest awhile and take in different vistas. All of these things add interest to the small space I have; after all, the garden is only 100′ x 200′, but it cannot be seen in a single glance because it has variety.

Just as gardening anywhere in America has its particular benefits and drawbacks, so gardening in Memphis, Tennessee, poses many challenges. In the winter we have the freeze-and-thaw syndrome to cope with: typically we will have unseasonably warm temperatures for a few weeks, followed by a cold snap. Azaleas, dogwoods, and yews especially are hurt by this kind of weather. In addition, we have an extremely fast growing season. We get lush, quick growth, but we have a short blooming period; our perennials bloom and fade without lingering. As a result I have found it necessary to place annuals in pots throughout the garden in order to sustain color all summer. The pots serve a dual purpose in providing not only color but also interesting shapes and varying levels in the garden.

The heat in summer is another matter altogether. From mid-June to mid-October I normally water from eight to ten hours a day just to keep things lush and moist. In the summer, because of all the watering I do, my garden is usually ten degrees cooler than my neighbors'.

How much work does all of this take? I usually spend twenty hours each week in the garden. Fortunately I am a morning person, so I start each day at around 5:00 A.M. I do light pruning, dead-heading, weeding, and tending. I have a gardener, M. J. Lunsford, who comes daily and does what I cannot do. In addition, a professional service manicures the lawn and grounds weekly.

I know that I will never be "finished" with my garden. If I ever do finish, I also know that it will be time to move on. My next goal is to build a temple out of Cotswold stone. If I die at a decent time of year (though I do not foresee my death in the immediate future), I want to be viewed in state in my temple, in my garden. This I would consider an appropriate end to a life spent happily in the garden.

Under the shade of a rare English hornbeam (*Carpinus betulus*), hostas, liriope, astilbe, sedum, and other shade-tolerant plants grow in front of the Gothic-style window. At the center of the bed is a Harewood House reproduction stone jardiniere planted with Boston ivy and cotoneaster.

Old-fashioned *Phlox paniculata*—"not my favorite color" for many, but one I like—blooms with *Rosa* 'Betty Prior'. The 'Ryan's White' chrysanthemum flowers here in July, the sturdiest, most drought-resistant of them all. With no dead-heading, plantlets appear in profusion on each stem and are easily propagated in water—instant gifts for those who stop by.

WHEN I BEGAN TO MAKE MY GARDEN in 1980, I was filled with thirty-five years' worth of inspirations and dreams. In that same year I visited Monet's garden at Giverny. This was the catalyst for my desire to express myself as an artist and to begin painting with flowers. How eager I was with a blank canvas, and how much I have learned! Through my own garden I have been able to recapture and relive all the enduring visions of my childhood and to integrate them into all that I have learned since I dug the first hole and scattered the first seeds at Le Jardin des Fleurs. After many ventures into ditch banks and deserted garden yards to gather seeds of disappearing plants, many swaps with gardening friends, many shipments from mail-order firms, and, most important, constant help from my dear friends at Goodness Grows and Heistaway Gardens, I think I have been able to create a fairly respectable cottage garden in the South.

Even as I write, and after several days of rain, the sun comes out again and birds are singing. I can take a walk and look at all that I have done and all that has been given to me. In just a while the fireflies will begin to flicker. Tomorrow I will be able to see the morning glories, but right now I have a four o'clock on my table that emits a fragrance full of memory and heart's desire.

The rooms of my small cottage are filled with very special objects—books, paintings, seeds, thoughts, and photographs of friends who have helped me in the garden ("Just outside my wisdom are the words that would answer everything")—and so is the garden: it is composed of rooms full of thoughts. There is the visitor's garden, the arbors, the stacked stone wall, the barn garden, the borders, the oval, the potager, the copse, and the sidewalks, all brimming with plants and flowers. There is topiary of a whimsical nature, garden seats, and knots-in-a-pot, rabbits made of vine for sweet peas to ramble through, standards of viburnum, cherry laurel, lantana, plumbago, roses, and box. No one aspect is so refined that it has lost or ever will lose its charm.

The plants themselves are as eclectic as my memory—good garden plants that need to be here in this setting. We have many natives, so important in the making of our gardens. True success comes from blending these with plants from other places, so that when certain colors, forms, and textures are combined, a good garden picture is made—a lasting memory.

Juniperus virginiana was used by Chuck Domermuth to create an arbor of simple peaks decreasing in height in a subtle forced perspective. In late September *Aster grandiflorus, Begonia grandis,* and my highly sought-after single pink chrysanthemum make walking through a memorable experience.

The house is draped with vine and clothed with climbers—so well draped and clothed that a frequent visitor once asked in surprise, "When did you get a house?" I replied, "It seemed somehow a necessity since I found myself living here."

There has been a gathering together, however, and there have been many lessons, all of which I have dutifully learned. I repeat certain plantings, I still cast out seed, and I am always willing to try new plants that will integrate themselves into my garden setting, but best of all that remains are those things that are in accordance with Nature herself. Is she not the greatest teacher? With her we can walk the garden path, whether it be in the woods or in a maze, taking the time to pause and enjoy a winter gaze: "When you walk in a garden the garden should walk with you." The best of all of this is creating a garden that blends into our own being, becoming what we see and feel and hold most dear.

The color scheme must be in accordance. We must be there in the moment when the light of day brings us a vista of pure delight and at night when the moon flowers open and in the morning when other flowers show forth their being. We must endure the drought and know that certain flowers come then and bear forth their beauty when Spring herself is fast asleep. And when Fall comes with leaves dancing down it is another vision of the rainbow that fills our dreams. Winter herself presents a scheme, and at Christmas we can adorn the house on its inside and celebrate the dream.

Left: Viewed from the upstairs porch, covered with *Parthenocissus tricuspidata*, is an arbor of *Vitis rotundifolia*, an aromatic experience in August, when grapes squeeze through bare toes. In the fall its golden-delicious-apple-yellow is rivaled by the canopy of *Ulmus alata*, whose winged branches make great supports for the sweet peas in late spring.

Wrought-iron garden furniture provides a sense of nostalgia for many Southerners who remember their grandmothers' terraces. A collection of hand-painted and natural terra-cotta pots holds *Parthenocissus henryi* and 'Yellow Princess' shrimp plants. The two standards are *Prunus caroliniana*, a native cherry laurel, one of my favorites for trimming into topiary.

Smith Hanes and I designed "Smith's Vegetable Garden" with a pattern of diamonds made of 'Winter Gem' buxus, planted with standards of *Rosa* 'The Fairy' and infilled with black-seeded Simpson lettuces, sown in situ, underplanted each spring with our choice of tulips—this year we selected 'Greenland'.

Opposite: The walk around the mixed borders features a glazed Italian urn in a bed of lady's mantle and annuals that change with the seasons. The pattern is made of coping used by the Holcombe family for "perennials" to supply cut flowers for the trade. Here in late August standards of *Hydrangea paniculata* 'Grandiflora' steal the scene, their white heads billowing like great massing clouds.

Now I will dutifully describe some of my garden settings and combinations and those particular plants that I love most dearly.

Macleaya, with its delightful plume that catches the wind on its underside, is superb in the borders, a great companion for the "exotic" grasses I have planted.

My standard *Hydrangea paniculata* 'Grandiflora' are a favorite in the border, as they offer such a clean breath of air on a summer's night in August. The hydrangeas are among the finest woody shrubs and there are at least ten species or cultivars in the garden, giving blues, whites, and pinks from May until September.

Cherry laurel, *Prunus caroliniana*, encloses the borders, which are sixty feet long and six feet deep. I keep several clipped forms throughout the garden, and though they require diligent trimming, their lustrous green foliage makes it worthwhile.

For the gardener in this region of the South there is an amazing group of drought-resistant plants worthy of mention throughout the garden. This list would include many annuals, but for those who desire good herbaceous perennials, I would suggest the following: *Rudbeckia fulgida* 'Goldsturm', *Leucanthemum* x *superbum* 'Ryan's White', *Artemisia* 'Huntingdon Gardens', *Verbena tenuisecta* 'Alba', *Phlox paniculata*, *Echinacea purpurea* (the improved forms and 'White Swan'), *Thalictrum delavayi*, *Veronicastrum*

virginicum 'Album', selections of lythrum, *Veronica* 'Icicle', *Boltonia asteroides* and *B.a.* 'Snowbank', *Lysimachia clethroides*, various monardas (especially the later-blooming forms), *Hosta ventricosa* and *H.* 'Royal Standard', and *Clematis indivisa* (syn. *C. paniculata*). For the summer garden there are many more I enjoy, and if these are combined with the annuals the garden will never want for bloom.

If there is any great reward for all the work involved in making a good garden, it is the pleasure of sharing. Many people might be at a loss for a gift for a friend or an unexpected visitor, but the greatest gift of all is a simple bouquet gathered from the garden. And a garden well planned will always give you that in return for the digging, snipping, and dead-heading, no matter the season. With it you could always write a poem or a thought.

This thought I give to you, the reader:

I gaze upon the garden
My heart grows peacefully still —
From its color comes my being,
From its spirit comes my will.

Harland J. Hand

I BUILT A LITTLE ROCK GARDEN when I was eight and at fourteen expanded it all the way down our "side hill" to the lake. This hillside was always my special place for playtime adventure. It was my Minnesota mountain, and I tried to make it a mountain garden adventure. But southern Minnesota is not kind to garden adventurers: the summers burn with 90° temperatures and hot winds, and winter brings bitter −20° days alternating with thaws that can turn the hardiest plants and the hardiest gardeners to mush. I ventured anyway.

In 1947, after a busy round of military service, college, and work, I visited San Francisco and was nearly undone by the marvels in my aunt Ellen's garden. Plants in seemingly endless variety grew with a vigor and substance I had never seen before. This had to be the perfect gardening climate: no destructive winds, cool summers and wet, usually frost-free winters, and then the hills—they were mountains! The very next year I moved to San Francisco to find a niche for myself. I helped with Aunt Ellen's garden and worked as a florist while finishing a B.A. and M.A. in art (with a minor in biology) at the University of California at Berkeley, and in 1952 I started teaching biology and physiology. Two years later I used my every resource to buy a steep El Cerrito hillside property. This would be my great mountain-adventure garden.

Here, just as in nature, succulents grow best in the company of other plants. Aloe and echeveria hybrids, *Crassula falcata*, and *Agave victoriae-reginae* mingle with azaleas, salvias, and roses. The combination is backed up by *Leptospermum* 'Ruby Glow' and a dwarf form of New Zealand flax (*Phormium tenax*).

Opposite: The tiny steps of an ascending "detail path" bring the visitor's eye close to the intricacies of *Azalea* 'Ward's Ruby' (with crane), aloe hybrids, *Echeveria elegans*, *Aeonium* 'Zwartkop', *Lithodora diffusa* 'Grace Ward', and flowering *Oxalis incarnata*.

The trickle falls drop with a splash as the red flowers of a *Kalanchoe blossfeldiana* hybrid (a common pot plant elsewhere) climb the "planter cliff." Bromeliads, leaves of cymbidium orchids, and succulent echeverias cascade down the cliff, with *Muehlenbeckia axillaris* filling the cracks between the rocks below.

A decaying, literally tumbledown house stood at the top of my southwest-facing, sandstone-ridge lot; this half-acre property, narrow and strewn with rocks, descended seventy-five feet in its 274 feet of length. I found no more than three feet of soil anywhere, one small pocket of adobe and the rest pure humus layered with shovel-defying rocks of all sizes. The remnants of a much-loved old garden occupied the top half, and a grove of forty eucalyptus trees the bottom half. Obsessed with the garden's possibilities, I hardly noticed the view—which included San Francisco Bay, four bridges, and twenty municipalities in seven counties.

Ten years passed before I could remodel the collapsing house. I fended off con-demnation proceedings and gloried in the garden, eliminating eucalyptus, changing contours, moving plants, and exposing large rocks and rearranging others.

I had never seen a garden do what I thought a garden ought to do. Nature was always the master garden designer: in nature things move, rivers flow, flowers grow where the wind scatters their seeds, rocks tumble down, the earth shifts, swells, and sags, action is evident everywhere. An infinity of adventures shows in every plant and time-worn rock, yet nature's compositions express the most profound serenity. Could one do better than to interpret this in a garden?

A teacher's income allows for minimum expenditures and maximum dedication. When time allowed, the same went into my garden. I learned to water efficiently—a new experience and one basic to dry-season California gardening. Because of the shallow soil, I also added over a hundred cubic yards of rich adobe topsoil. Then there were the rocks, "too small to use," unearthed every time I swung the pickax.

Paths were among my earliest problems. The cheapest material was concrete (dis-

POETS AND PAINTERS

appearing gravel would not do, and flat rocks were costly). I tried making stepping stones by sculpting wet concrete with a trowel. My first attempts produced a nice flowing curve, and that curve plus the color of the concrete reminded me of my favorite place in all nature—the gray granite glacial washes of the high Sierras. I tried to capture in concrete what I had felt in that powerful and dramatic place, sculpting steps, stepping stones, large slabs, and then ponds, boulder benches, and stratified planters. I used the smallest "useless rocks" under the slabs and the largest piled together to form the core of each bench; this saved concrete and, I found out later, strengthened it.

The concrete structures became "bedrock" over which the native rocks appeared to tumble. The structures flowed into varied curved trails that widened into sheltering "rooms," past lookouts over the bay or over other parts of the garden. I wanted ponds to give the garden the engraved look of a dry riverbed with remnant water here and there. The concept of "here and there" resulted in nineteen ponds.

At the time of writing, there are twelve shelterlike rooms of various sizes among wandering trails involving two hundred steps. At the bottom of the garden a bulldozer and a jackhammer dug out the largest and most spectacular room, sixty feet across and forty feet wide. On the upside is a cliff ten feet high, stratified with concrete planters; it is divided by two rather grand staircases that descend toward each other. A pond at the top of the cliff has a trickle waterfall that splashes into another pond below; the waterfall's sound and movement are intensified by the curving of the cliff. Opposite the falls, three ponds cluster to separate two viewing benches that carry the eye to the far edges of the garden. I want the eye to flow easily over the garden, never feeling compelled either to move or to stop.

Concrete steps climb through a sheltering ravine and out into an "alpine meadow." A native rock outcrop is filled with cascading cymbidium orchids, which dominate this area from December to May. The conifer in the foreground is *Chamaecyparis pisifera* 'Filifera.'

My "art conditioning" in abstract expressionism helps me to see even familiar objects as moving, expressive shapes. This makes composing the garden an intriguing delight, with every installation an experiment in composition. I make changes wherever I can visualize improvements—I have redesigned staircases that were boring or too steep, and whole sections have been torn up and redone. My test for rightness of composition is in the maintenance: if I pull the weeds and keep things pruned, the area is right. If nature can continuously recompose, why can't I?

The plants appear to thrive and triumph in the microclimates of the concrete structures. Hundreds of feet of crevices (from wet to dry) hold little plants such as thyme, bellis, muscari. The crevices—ready-made cracks that allow for the movement of a restless hillside—exist because the concrete structures are separated by at least two inches of soil. Among the rooms and paths stand plant "islands." Each is a "flower arrangement" with tall plants placed off-center, surrounded by shorter ones and with low ones around the edges (nature does it that way, too). I want the "island flower arrangements" to move with the composition of the whole garden. Trees, shrubs, annuals, and perennials all thrive and move together—or seem to, with a little judicious pruning.

Although excess water runs down the steps and off the garden, I cherish both wet and dry places as special plant habitats. Japanese iris flourish in drainage runs, and in places skipped by the sprinklers grow agaves, aloes, and California natives. Ground orchids, tree ferns, and most succulents even naturalize in wet, well-drained niches. Varying intensity of shade comes from a few coastal live oaks, whose rambling branches hold epiphytic orchids (laelias, oncidiums, and so on) among staghorn ferns and bromeliads. The branches drip in the remarkable cloud-forest conditions of our San Francisco fog, and tall flames of reed orchids flower continuously in the full sun of this "high tropic" environment.

Right now there are some two thousand varieties of plants growing in the garden

Echeveria 'Afterglow' thrives in the company of lamb's ears (*Stachys byzantina*), *Oxalis incarnata*, and yellow-flowered sparaxis.

(I estimate that another two thousand dried up, froze, got crowded out, or gave up). Some I collected in the high tropics; others were gifts or purchases from nurseries wherever I have traveled. Rare plants are soon shared so they are less likely to be lost; my cutting yard is full of plants to install or share.

New plants wait to be organized into the color patterns of the garden. The dominant color theme is established by the light-gray of the concrete structures against the darker colors of plants and native rock. It is this contrast that helps to give the Sierran glacial washes their power and drama, and the same contrast dominates the view from the garden. California light is bright and clear, bringing strong color contrast to everything (cypress trees, for instance, have golden highlights with black shadows), and this contrast also serves to create pure, jewel-like colors that go together in marvelously unexpected ways, often puzzling to first-time visitors from other climates.

Each area of the garden has a predominant color. For example, the section below the house is white with wisteria, waterlilies, roses, heuchera, iberis, camellias, cymbidiums, heather, Shasta daisies, calla lilies, and magnolia. A touch of yellow from abutilon, azaleas, and *Achillea tomentosa* gives richness and subtlety, and the dark foliage of yew and hinoki cypress (a grove of seven, dwarfed to six or seven feet) brightens the whites. I once tried adding very dark reds and blues instead, but the whites were not brightened nearly so well. The edge of the white garden invades and is invaded on one side by the heat of oranges, reds, and pinks, and on the other by cooler pinks and reds. I use bits of blue and violet to intensify warmer colors and touches of orange, red, or yellow to brighten cool colors.

The gray leaves of *Stachys byzantina*, grasses, and succulents soften and enlarge the gray shapes of the concrete when planted next to them. Pale white, yellow, pink, and lavender flowers also dot and dash light color across the "islands" or mass together in gentle repose.

A "red island" has *Magnolia* x *soulangeana* 'Rustica Rubra', rhododendrons 'Radium' and 'Cornubia', azalea 'Ward's Ruby', and the roses 'Better Times' and 'Garnet', the latter a dark red. In spring the area is a glorious red on red, but soon only the roses are left for color. And what color! It takes the red of only one 'Better Times' rose to light up a whole "island" of green—the dark green of rhododendrons and azaleas, the medium green of magnolia, and the light yellow-green of Japanese boxwood. Against these "lighted-up" greens, the rose-red of 'Better Times' in turn sings out in perfect coloratura.

With every season comes a change of mood, as light and colors come and go. Even in the rain, the garden has moods that touch me—it is the only time when I cannot work in the garden. Frost comes rarely, and once in the last forty years we have had a freeze that slaughtered plants I loved, but I do not grieve. Nor do I grieve for the great sheltering golden willow just killed by oak-root fungus. In the garden I feel wonderful powers: I am an adventurer, I play nature, I make changes, I start over, I introduce new things. I even play nature's succession: I move the earth, I start with annuals, I end with trees. I compose, I recompose. Sometimes when I do these things I think that those who indulge in the "art of the garden" are gods, or something like them. But then, is that not true of all those who work with the magic of nature's disciplines?

Japanese cranes chase butterflies in the succulent garden set with the black-leaved *Aeonium* 'Zwartkop', an aloe hybrid, and red crassulas; masses of *Echeveria elegans* suggest the cascading flow of a stream in the background. Festuca grasses, red azaleas, and other nonsucculents mix in.

THE GARDEN OF

Robert Dash

MADOO

SAGAPONACK, NEW YORK

THE GARDENING ART is a constantly amended, infinitely variable essay on green—green rising into the sky, green rising through the earth, green puncturing water or shown on top of it. Green is the proper livery of the garden, and all the rest is nonessential bedeckment. I would as soon have a so-called white garden as I would a pink lawn or a black tomato.

If it is executed in an impeccable manner, gardening becomes one of the fine arts. Like sculpture or dance, it moves in the empty air and gives it substance. Yet to be fine, a garden must seem effortless—no matter how much art and thought and pain and effort go into the task. "As you rise in the world, you sink the accomplishment," said Henry James. Gardening is, all told, a highly unnatural act. A fine garden sits not in a direct line from Nature, but to one side of it, like some splendid apple on the ground in a windfall, often far from the tree. In creating a garden, one must often run counter to Nature, the true spirit of the place being the perspicacity and wisdom and spiritual strength of the gardener, rather than the place itself or the earth on which he works—that is no more than a blank canvas.

What my role is in all of this I do not know. I took up gardening quite early on, my first memory being the image of my mother in white—white dress, white hat, white gloves—bending over iris, a kind of imprinting no one could ever flee from. The fact that my mother has suggested that nobody ever gardened in white gloves does not fudge the image. It is mine.

In the spring of 1966, frayed by working and living in a studio in a bottle-strewn part of downtown New York City, tired of renting places for the summer months where I would dig and delve and then leave it all for others, I struck out and found a plot of 1.91 acres at the far eastern tip of Long Island, surrounded by potato fields, in sight of the Atlantic Ocean. What I purchased was a lush sweep of unmown field grass without a single tree or bush, on which stood a large barn built of shipwreck timber in 1740, with a subsidiary one attached, itself built some hundred years later, and a milk house and crib house of late eighteenth-century vintage. Out of these gray, weathered shingle structures I made two houses and two painting studios, one for winter, one for summer. In them I have been living and working ever since.

In 1967 I started a small garden of nothing much. It was a disorderly mixture of herbs and vegetables, mostly, with asparagus gone to plume weaving in and out to give some sort of linear definition. What paths there were consisted of tinted concrete setts plunked down on the alluvial-outwash earth and moved out of the way of a plant when it wanted to take over. The rest of the property I kept to grass, mowing it in broad six-foot strips to make walkways in whatever pattern I wished. They curved and hawked

A quiet corner of the garden, enclosed and sheltered on all sides by the house, gives views from inside and out. A June mix of yarrow and *Astilbe* 'Deutschland' sweeps toward a pillared rose, 'Dortmund'. Clematis, roses, spires of *Asphodel* 'Lutea', and *Miscanthus sinensis* create a medley of colors in a densely planted cottage style.

Opposite: The feathers of plume poppy shag over a wash of sidalcea seen from the roof deck in summer. The poppy is stripped of its lower leaves to a height of six feet to reveal the gray-blue stems; the sidalcea is cut to the ground after flowering for a second display.

Stripped of laterals and leaves, that ordinary mule of a hedge, privet, is transformed into a grace of gray trunks supporting shaggy, unclipped heads. The ground cover is woodruff (*Galium odoratum*).

A late-nineteenth-century Korean export jar, holding a bouquet of bamboo stakes to be used as needed, stands next to an eighteenth-century millstone found on the property. The umbels of *Allium giganteum* and second-year leeks line the tinted concrete sets of the path.

back, seeming never to reach a door, rather like the random tracks of a hay wagon driven home by a sleepy old ox. It was all green against gray under a sky most often as milky as some pilgrim's gruel, well suited to the area's history, since it was settled in 1656 by people from Kent, some of whose descendants still live and farm just down the road from me.

All well and good, but then I began to wish for trees to blunt the corrosive Atlantic winds. For privacy, too. (My gates read "No Callers.") I began reaching out from the houses and in from the property lines, thinking of it all in sculptural, not painterly, terms, and especially of the moment when the trees might tower over what I had built. I was nowhere near where I wanted to be in gardening skills then, and still am not, the huge subject being one that enlarges the longer one goes at it. What the garden

One of three artificial ponds, five and a half feet deep at the center, with native waterlilies in bloom. In autumn, the opposite shore is a burnish of goldenrod and tansy.

The "view-swiper" is 120 feet long and, to reinforce the perspective, narrows from eight to six feet at the far end, the better to bring the outlying potato fields within the confines of the garden. The Rugosa rose 'Fru Dagmar Hastrup' lines both sides. The foreground oval of yews will be clipped flat.

was then and always will be for me, however, is a form of autobiography, one that unmistakably reveals the errors of my character. It is even capable of admonition.

I am an extremely impromptu kind of person, the sort who plunges in first and thinks and redoes afterward. Advice never sinks in. My procedure in gardening is thus full of the wildest starts and incompletions, a long succession of blunders before the thing comes right. Although at times I have been on target at first go, this is rare. Even a simple ornamental bowl will have to travel the length and breadth of the garden for a year or more before it finds its inescapably proper perch. Add to the above the fact that I am easily bored, and it may be that I am someone who should not garden at all.

I find that giving marks to my two decades of garden making is rather like staring into a mirror and being alternately pleased and irritated. I do believe, though, that this garden succeeds when my hand is not too visible, when an imperative richness becomes prominent, when a saunter through it becomes a comfort and not an apology. There are many ways of going through the garden, and I like to watch visitors doing so, following their own agenda. From them I learn, just as I do from those all-too-frequent windows made by storms. Gardening is a description of the very air, however.

I know that my garden will never be completed—that is the very dynamic of the activity. However distinctive they may be, gardens never get signed as paintings do. Even so, at this moment it has certain distinctions that have stood the test of time in a possibly individual way, and some of these I should like to list:

An unusual way of pruning has reshaped two rows of privet so that their trunks are bare to a height of eight feet and more, above which they bloom and shag in the wind with an odor a bit like vanilla, a sad vanilla far away from the orchid seed. It allows air and light to shuttle through and avoids that claustrophobia the small garden is often prone to. It is understoried with woodruff and mints and the smallest of spring bulbs.

Toward the winter house, the earthen pile tossed by the excavators has been shaped into a berm with an apical channel to collect rainwater. It is clothed in unpruned Arctic willow and ostrich fern held at the base by native rhododendron. The whole mound operates like a wick, and it all does very well indeed.

If I do not much care for strong floral color, I like my fences, posts, gates, benches, and railings rather hot. These and the houses and studios sport mixtures of musty blues and several greens and many yellows. The gazebo sums it all up, with two roofs in two shades of palest mauve topping a base of strong, shocking plum.

A meadow garden with an irregular center of grass is filled with monarda, various thalictrums, *Rosa rugosa* 'Blanc Double de Coubert', milkweed, tall and short Joe Pye weed, about twelve varieties of solidago, peony 'Festiva Maxima', thistles, and much more; it continues to be a cynosure.

Tall matter is at the edges. The wind constantly parts the clumps to where, toward the center, smaller things may be seen. And then not seen.

I have enlarged my three ponds and two bridges by placing mirrors in the nearby shed.

There is much else in the garden, but they are things that I think need amendment and are not quite right yet. A narrow spur of land that ends the garden is all right, however. On it is a long brick path flying out to the potato fields and the ocean, narrowing toward its tip (from eight feet to six) and lined at the sides with *Rosa rugosa* 'Fru Dagmar Hastrup', a color seemingly made by the bricks or echoing them.

Another berm marks the west side of the garden, packed with broom, red- and yellow-twigged dogwood, and whatever of robust habit has overflowed from elsewhere. Here birds and opossum and fox and, alas, rabbits take their roam, rather remindful of the early days of this town and of my first view of this property, when it was all random grass and a few shingled barns.

N EWCOMERS TO OUR GARDEN must find it very odd, because after twenty-five years it is still unfinished—a mixture of successes, failures being revised, and groups of stakes (sometimes color-coded) to be studied for a season or two in developing new areas. We do have a master plan, however. New additions proceed when we are satisfied with the design refinement and as time and funds permit. We are in no hurry: creation and refinement are each a source of pleasure.

At the head of this west-to-east stream valley there are grades steep enough to provide two levels and a variety of exposures on which to garden. Near the top of the valley is a two-story fieldstone-and-frame springhouse, circa 1860, which is a principal garden ornament. These two "givens" have strongly influenced the informal character of the garden, as has the one-story house built twenty-five years ago to serve as a bridge across the stream.

It soon became apparent that in order to respond properly to the challenging nature of the site, there should be a series of garden experiences with a very strong linkage—what I like to call an American stroll garden. Because of my own artistic proclivities, the style needed to be clearly of this century. As a result, two of the small, scarce level areas have decidedly Mondrian-like patterns; one of these is also strongly influenced by early-twentieth-century Danish garden design. The balance of the garden is for the most part free-form (admittedly influenced by the work of Roberto Burle Marx), carefully studied both to relate to existing land contours and to create carefully structured open spaces.

While the rectilinear areas could safely be jumbled with vegetables (in one case) and flowers (in the other), disciplined by a color scheme and seasonal emphasis, I knew that for the free-form areas plants had to serve as structure, both vertically and horizontally. The latter meant painting with large brushstrokes, as in the planting of the thirty-five *Forsythia* 'Spring Glory' and fifty each of three cultivars of French lilacs that create the space through which the entrance drive passes.

To this design objective had to be wedded my lifelong love of and curiosity about plants and my philosophical commitment to have an "exuberant garden." I feel that in an age of high-pressure living gardens must be more captivating and full of charm and magic

Tulips ('Uncle Tom', 'Beauty of Apeldoorn', 'Queen Wilhelmina', and 'West Point') and *Myosostis* 'Victoria Blue' create a Mondrian-like pattern in the studio garden.

Japanese long-flowered wisteria, *Wisteria floribunda* 'Royal Purple' (foreground), 'Rosea' (middle ground), and 'Alba' (background), have been trained for over thirty-five years as trees. Fastened to a well-anchored galvanized pipe, the vines are allowed to branch only at three-foot intervals in order to provide an uncrowded display of flowers.

In April a Burle Marxian, broad brushstroke of *Forsythia* x *intermedia* 'Spring Glory' is seen through the branches of river birch (*Betula nigra*). Along with American holly (*Ilex opaca*), the birch provides the structure of the winter garden. In the foreground is Japanese cornelian cherry (*Cornus officinalis*), whose flowers start opening even before the forsythia's.

than ever before—strong medicine, as it were. This meant taking great care to avoid having a horticultural zoo.

Planting has proceeded at a pretty steady pace for twenty-five years. We have had our share of setbacks in the course of learning about our site and becoming educated about plant requirements. A mass planting of *Corylopsis glabrescens*, which was supposed to hang its green-yellow tassels with the waxy white cups of Yulan magnolia, got frosted in bud or bloom for seven years running, and finally a dramatic climatic shift—bringing winter temperature to −14° in 1983–84 and 1984–85—killed the wood. A grove of golden-chain trees prospered long enough to encourage us to complete the planting of the Ghent azalea, *Rhododendron* x *gandavense* 'Coccinea Speciosa', beneath them; the trees then promptly contracted canker and died. A group of seven or eight koelreuterias, after reaching semimaturity, suddenly decided to express their regrets over our clay soil and depart.

The corylopsis were removed and replaced by a completely new scheme featuring a persimmon grove and other plants that will stand tough winter, dry soil, and clay conditions. Selecting a replacement for the laburnums was a head-scratcher, but we finally settled on *Cornus florida* 'Hohman's Golden', the foliage of which is a wonderful chartreuse just as the azaleas blow orange, and later in the season it makes a charming picture with the deep-apricot *Hemerocallis* 'Aten'. The elimination of the koelreuterias proved to be a

POETS AND PAINTERS

blessing, as it provided the extra space needed for a winter garden, which was itself larger than originally anticipated.

Thirteen *Wisteria floribunda* cultivars trained as twelve-foot trees have, on the other hand, flourished since we moved them onto our hottest, driest hillside. They have been so successful, in fact, that our original plans were altered to feature a wisteria walk culminating in two giant "trees" (wisteria vines, that is, trained on Corten steel frames), one of shade-tree shape and twenty feet tall, the other of conifer shape and thirty-five feet tall.

We have had similar success with shrub roses (mostly old-timers). High on the same hillside with the wisterias, where the air circulation is excellent, they were planted in deeply prepared soil and took off. I will never forget one Sunday morning the second June after planting. I was up early and caught the scent from the bottom of the valley. As I proceeded uphill (on a zigzag route), I literally moved through a whole series of different and intoxicating fragrances until, when really among them, I was in a state of euphoria.

Gardens give of their best, of course, when shared with others. An event in 1986 illustrates a serendipitous example. The centerpiece of our garden is the stream that, early on, our landscape architect friend Conrad Hamerman converted to a landscape of beautiful ponds and waterfalls. This water garden begins, at the highest elevation, with a circular pond surrounded by vertical evergreens (*Juniperus virginiana* and *Sciadopitys verticillata*), which has always captivated me with its special intimacy, its marsh marigolds in May, and its velvety clump of mauve-purple *Iris ensata* var. *spontanea* in June. On a sunny, breezy day in early May the garden had been opened for the benefit of a local charity. Those running the affair turned up with a string quartet; because it was too windy

Below left: These steps provide access to a garden of long-flowered Japanese *Wisteria floribunda* trained on frames as trees; they pass through a ground cover of wine-colored foliage, *Berberis thunbergii* 'Crimson Pygmy'. The self-seeded ox-eye daisies (*Leucanthemum vulgare*) are serendipitous.

A grove of golden dogwood (*Cornus florida* 'Hohman's Golden') supplies chartreuse foliage at the moment in May when orange Ghent and Mollis azaleas bloom. The grove is structured by four incense cedars (*Calocedrus decurrens*) and backed by the wine-colored foliage of beech trees (*Fagus sylvatica* 'Riversii').

Opposite: Life-size sculptures of three of the owners' children greet visitors as they ascend to the Game Lawn. The view is from the upper pond, which is surrounded by vertical evergreens (Eastern red cedar [*Juniperus virginiana*] on the left, umbrella pine [*Sciadopitys verticillata*] on the right). The azalea is *Rhododendron* (Gable Hybrid) 'Stewartstonian'.

The ponds in the stream valley garden; the man-made island is at upper left. The ponds were built among existing mature trees, but none was lost because the water level of each pond was set not to exceed that of the original stream in relation to adjacent trees.

to manage sheet music on the open lawn, I suggested that the musicians move to the shelter of this upper pond. To our great surprise and the delight of all our visitors, this turned out to be an exquisite open-air music room and a perfect sound box for sending music down the valley to the house.

A similar numinous moment occurred one July evening as we gathered at dining tables by our swimming pool and its grape-clad arbor to celebrate the forthcoming wedding of our son and daughter-in-law. As the sun settled behind the hills, a kindly light touched all the nearby grasses and bamboos; just as we were lighting candles for the climax of the celebration, the moon rose round and yellow. Gardens are settings for living, and there is nothing like their magic spell when all is right.

Of course, the greatest satisfaction of having a garden is the one-on-one involvement it brings with other gardeners. I cannot end without noting my gratitude to some of the many friends who have shared plants, saved me from bungling mistakes, comforted me in moments of failure, and rejoiced with me when things worked well: Tom Williams, our first gardener; Conrad Hamerman; that horticultural standard-bearer Dick Lighty; a philosopher and plantsman extraordinaire, the late Hal Bruce; Barry Yinger, bearer of treasures from the Orient; Tom Buchter; and Paul Skibinski, my present gardener, who always seems to know what the plants are thinking before I do.

Tall sea grapes (*Coccoloba uvifera*) screen the entrance court where *Datura arborea* and African iris are blooming. A staghorn fern grows on bark attached to the arbor.

Concrete Aztec figures cloaked in *Ficus pumila* guard the lagoon at the back of the garden, while a friendly great gray heron keeps a keen lookout for fish at the shallow edges of the water. Mangrove and Brazilian pepper trees rim the water, providing complete privacy.

I AM AN ARCHITECT AND DESIGNER of interiors and furniture. When I design a residence, I like to design the garden as well as the architecture and the interiors. In fact I can never think "house" without thinking "garden"—the two must complement each other and create a whole design. My training sees to that, so all the gardens I have made have a strong architectural quality. The basic elements for house and garden are the same: the designer deals with the relation of positives and negatives, solids and voids, open spaces and enclosures, light and shadow, textures and colors; the gardener deals with these, too, but has the added delights of sound and the changing sky above.

I have created a garden wherever I have lived—in Alabama, Chicago, Long Island, and Florida. The older I get, the less I need and want, and so my gardens get smaller along with my own capacities, but they still provide what I require. The first and most important thing is privacy—the greatest luxury. It is not easy to attain in this country, where walls and fences are frowned upon and where one is expected to continue the strip of grass across the front of the property, joining similar strips on either side. Approved planting is not along the street but along the foundation of the house— something I hate.

When I decided to make Florida my winter headquarters, I settled on Sarasota, on the Gulf of Mexico, because it has beautiful beaches of hard-packed white sand (excellent for walking on), affords easy access by air to all parts of the country, and offers opportunities for an active life in all the arts. So after a test period during which I rented, I started looking for a place in which to live and work from November to May.

After weeks of searching, I found the place I ended up buying—a designer's nightmare, giving new meaning to the word *challenge*. Yet it met my basic requirements, which included a southern orientation of the side away from the street. It was in a very good neighborhood on an island connected by bridges to the mainland on one end and to Siesta Key on the other. This key is one of the oldest residential areas in Sarasota, and the nearby village provides the necessities, plus the greatest beach for walking to be found anywhere in the world—a long crescent with hard-packed white sand and the "crystal waters" of the Gulf of Mexico.

Directly behind the property to the south is a sizable pond fed by water that comes through a narrow channel from the bay. This pond is rimmed with mangrove trees that can never be cut: their exposed roots provide homes for water creatures and a parade ground for herons and other water birds. Families of red mullet leap into the air and skip across the water like flat round stones. In the distance, rising above the ring of mangroves, is a single, very tall Washingtonia palm that looks as though it must be hanging on a

string attached in the sky. It is the most flexible tree I have ever seen and has withstood the strength of gale-force winds.

When I bought the place there was no semblance of a garden. The yard had a single tree—a miserable thing called a "mother-in-law's tongue" (*Albizia lebbeck*) because its dried pods rattle in the breeze—and a few crotons, which I detest. These were the first to go, then the tree. I was left with a clean slate.

Most of the yard available for making a garden was on the long side of the house, to the west, with a narrow strip of yard on the east. I promptly put up six-foot-high wooden stockade fences on both of these property lines. The driveway cut across the strip I wanted to make into a garden, so I moved it and created a new wide parking area between the street and the house; I paved this with gray stones and planted three royal palms, roystonea, on one side. To lead from this area into the garden, I designed a pair of metal gates flanked by bottomless cubes of cypress, and I planted ficus trees in these, with lavender lantana trailing over the sides of the boxes.

My next step was to take out all the grass, which requires far too much maintenance in the sandy soil of Florida, and to pave all of the traffic areas in concrete with exposed aggregate, leaving places for planting all the way to the water. A very private entrance court was created by extending the wall of the garage to the property line and planting a

Flanking the monogrammed metal gates are cypress boxes filled with weeping lantana around trimmed *Ficus benjamina* trees. Inside the entrance court, areca palms stand in raised boxes with a Queen Sago palm behind. *Thunbergia grandiflora* covers the fence with its sky-blue flowers.

SEASIDE, MOUNTAIN, DESERT

wide band of sea grape (*Coccoloba uvifera*) at the narrow end toward the street. One plant bed was filled with aspidistra. *Ficus pumila* grows on the new wall, with a band of liriope along the base, and raised cypress planters are furnished with areca palms. Kept trimmed at the bottom, these palms look rather like my favorite plant, bamboo; at their base, dwarf Confederate jasmine (*Jasminum nitidum*) hangs down to the ground around the boxes. One tall Phoenix palm adds to the tropical feeling, and a clump of datura provides fragrance on still nights.

Beyond the entrance court is a second courtyard outside the main guest bedroom. This is mostly paved, with large pots of calamondin oranges and a sort of Persian gazebo with cushions. Behind this are more areca palms in planters and a bed with rhapis palms and fatshedera on the fence.

On the other side of this courtyard is the longest plant bed, which extends the length of the house, all the way to the water. Along the walkway next to the house are pots of jade plant (*Crassula arborescens*) and African iris. Outside the side entrance to the living room, the paved walk ends in a wooden arbor, which is completely covered in April by the fragrant flowers of Confederate jasmine. Surrounded by pink crinum lilies and pots of yellow Carolina jasmine, *Gelsemium sempervirens*, this is a perfect place to have lunch in early spring—the friendly great blue herons often join us and gulp down any food they are offered.

The largest area of the garden is between the back of the house and the water. It is mostly paved, with narrow plant beds at the sides and bottomless cypress planters holding lovely blue-green *Cupressus leylandii* underplanted with dwarf jasmine. The four central planters with Texas sage are set at the corners of a raised platform with low chairs—a

The walled inner courtyard provides a private outdoor space for the guest room, which opens onto it. The Persian-inspired gazebo is a comfortable place to relax in the sunshine and enjoy the fragrance of calamondin orange blossoms.

At the rear of the house, the sitting platform overlooking the still water of the lagoon is supported at its four corners by cypress planters containing Texas sage surrounded by small-leaved Confederate jasmine. The small tree in the foreground is loquat (*Eriobotrya japonica*).

favorite place for watching the sea birds and the jumping mullet or the giant Washingtonia silhouetted in the moonlight.

The narrow strip along the east side of the house has single white hibiscus, schefflera and elephant ears, and a row of flue liners with liriope. An arbor outside the kitchen has more yellow Carolina jasmine, blooming fragrantly in late winter. A mockingbird likes to sing from an aerial above this small dining area, which is a delightful place to have breakfast.

Gardening in this part of Florida certainly has its problems. The soil is very sandy, so nutrients must be provided often. There are some winters when the temperature drops below freezing for a day or two—just long enough to kill the more tropical plants. Then there are occasional severe storms, with high tides and water rising over the entire yard. Planting in raised boxes helps, but the salt water takes its toll—I have had to start almost from scratch several times.

Each time this happens, I replace tropical plants such as loquat and mangoes with native plants such as wax myrtle (*Myrica cerifera*) and Brazilian pepper (*Schinus terebinthifolius*) that can take the cold and the salty water. So, like every garden I have ever had, my Florida garden is constantly changing. But the only thing we can count on in life is change—I find this one of the fascinating aspects of gardening.

My garden is a place to find peace and calm, a relief from the chaos and confusion created by man. By day it is filled with sunshine sparkling on the water; by night the fragrance of datura and jasmine hangs over it in the quiet, and I am reluctant to leave it to the moonlight.

Andrew Pierce

EVERGREEN, COLORADO

Penstemon pinifolius and a form of *Dianthus chinensis* create the foreground of this mixed area, which is highlighted by a native *Juniperus communis*.

H IGH UP ON THE HILLSIDE, tucked in among fairly mature specimens of Ponderosa pine and Douglas fir, is a small garden surrounding a modest house with views westward toward the high ranges of the Colorado Rockies. At approximately 14,260 feet, Mount Evans is the most prominent peak; close by are its neighbors, Bierstadt and Goliath. Visitors to the garden must drive thirty miles from Denver, gaining over two thousand feet in elevation; the last half mile consists of a series of switchbacks, and it seems that most of the gain is achieved in that short distance. Gardening here at 7,400 feet does have its problems, especially with the limited growth season, but we have taken the challenge and created a plantsman's garden.

In Colorado, at this elevation and with limited precipitation—perhaps twenty inches in a good year—seasonal growth of trees is diminished. They may reach fifty feet only after a couple of hundred years, and often they have shorter, heavier branch systems than trees at lower altitudes. Ponderosa pine makes a scattered forest that creates sun and shade patterns, so that most of the garden receives some sun every day—we never have the effect found in the eastern woodland, where in the height of summer all sunshine is literally blocked out. Of course, since we are so high up, the ultraviolet rays are more intense, and with good culture, fertilizer, and judicious watering, perennials—the backbone of the mountain garden—can put on excellent growth over a period of perhaps eighty frost-free days.

Mountain soil, or the lack of it, influences the type and style of gardening we carry out on the 25-degree, west-facing slope. Over the years, the continual addition of large amounts of organic material has made the soil much more water-retentive and has also allowed the roots to penetrate deeply, seeking any moisture available.

The pocket-handkerchief-sized lawn we have established on the west side of the house gives us a sheltered, shady sitting area and delineates the surrounding mixed perennial and annual border. Such marvelous items as *Dicentra spectabilis*, *Aquilegia triternata* and others, *Stachys officinalis*, and phalaris grass flourish in the nearby evergreen shade. Farther along the border, in the sunnier spots, *Delphinium elatum*, *Lychnis chalcedonica*, *Veronica longifolia* 'Blue Giant', *Helenium hoopesii*, *Thermopsis caroliniana*, *Dictamnus albus*, and the striking orange poppy 'Allegro' provide a background for the lowlier annuals and shorter perennials. Drifting the annuals seems to be most effective here, and against the heavier green of the background conifers one can better appreciate the subtler flowers of snapdragon, godetia, clarkia, calm-colored petunias, and softer marigolds. The style changes with the seasons, and with plenty of encouragement after their planting in June, the annuals reach their full glory quite rapidly.

Near the lawn a small vegetable garden helps supply our summer needs. We tend to

The small lawn is accented by groups of snapdragons on the raised planting area, which is backed and partially shaded by the natural woodland of Ponderosa pine and Douglas fir. Mixed perennials fill spaces at the back, with *Veronica longifolia* 'Blue Giant' predominating.

concentrate on such hardies as peas, spinach, leeks, brassicas, lettuces, onions, and carrots; we do grow beans, but in the shortest season these occasionally fail to mature. In certain years July is the only frost-free month.

Cultivation is possible on all four sides of the house, and even the rugged primula border on the north side shows how to capture the charm of a group of plants not often seen in our dry Colorado climate. Indeed, the state can boast only a few natives in this group—one from upper montane streamsides, and two rarer ones from wet meadow areas at nine to ten thousand feet. *Primula parryi*, from the streamside, grows in the peaty organic bed near the faucet, where it gets an ample water supply. Most prolific among the other species are drumstick primulas, *P. denticulata*, and—an influence from my youth in England—cowslips *P. elatior*, which have to be thinned out yearly. *P. auricula*, *P. japonica*, *P. pulverulenta*, and *P. florindae* add an exotic touch.

Following the rampage of the bulldozer when the house was built, we took the opportunity to reposition some large rocks; one of them, in the eight- to ten-ton range, holds an impressive display of sempervivum (hen-and-chickens) on its hollowed-out surface. In other areas small rocks have been carefully placed to build dry stone walls for retaining purposes. Native flora—*Sedum lanceolatum*, *Campanula rotundifolia*, artemisia, and *Corydalis aurea*—adorn these walls, along with such introductions as *Lewisia cotyledon* and *L. tweedyi*. Mountain air suits them and they produce specimens almost like cabbages.

SEASIDE, MOUNTAIN, DESERT

Lewisia was named after the nineteenth-century explorers and plantsmen Lewis and Clark; this little genus also gives us the Montana state flower, *L. rediviva*, which is elsewhere less easy to grow. Colorado's *L. pygmaea* is just that, a pygmy, and is often overlooked.

Natural rocks are an asset not available to most gardeners, and while several on the site formed the basis for a reasonably large rock garden, we added local granite rocks to create planter beds. Indeed, it is difficult to tell now which were imported and which are natural. Soil mixture here was amended with quantities of organic material (1 part to 3 parts of the native broken-granite soil gravel mix), improving the water retention and also allowing the root penetration that so many alpines desire. Foundation features were made with a few shrubs, such as *Daphne* x *burkwoodii* 'Somerset', existing local currant, *Ribes cereum*, and another Colorado native from the southern part of the state, *Cercocarpus ledifolius*, the curly-leaved mahogany.

The rock garden is more of a collector's paradise than an area that concentrates on any one genus. Gentians create lovely splashes of blue in summer, but spring is the alpine rock garden's moment. Very early on in the season *Synthyris missurica* establishes a bold splash of blue spikes among shiny, almost round, leaves. At the same time the early crocus are blooming and the first of several types of muscari are coming into beauty. Not far behind them, the Japanese *Potentilla megalantha* pushes up its fuzzy, white-edged foliage before the crystal-clear yellow flowers appear.

The rush is now on, and the ground-hugging *Phlox caespitosa pulvinata*, from high in the Rockies, becomes a mass of sweet-scented, light-blue, delicately petaled flowers. Arabis, aubrieta, and aurinia (syn. *Alyssum saxatile*) follow, and dwarf iris and tulips push their heads high, often amid the last snows of spring. Penstemons—which seem typically western—exhibit themselves in June, and the whole range of dianthi covers larger areas than one might wish: from maiden pinks (*Dianthus deltoides*) and minute *D. simulans*, a real mound, to *D. alpinus* and finally, in August, the unusual *D. knappii*, which, in contrast to most, has sulfur-yellow flowers.

Looking across the clumps of *Veronica longifolia* 'Blue Giant' and goldenrod toward the rock garden on the southeastern side of the house.

Scarlet runner beans grow profusely in the vegetable garden during the short summer season, producing beautiful flowers as well as useful fruit.

The main perennial areas on the warm south side of the house feature such mainstays as phlox, solidago, veronica, and *Sedum spectabile* 'Indian Chief'. More unusual are *Ligularia dentata* 'Desdemona', *Scabiosa caucasica* 'Miss Willmott', and *Malva alcea fastigiata*.

One of the attention-getting mid- to late-season bulbs is allium; with careful planning these can extend the flowering season quite considerably. Bright-blue, yellow, deep purple, and rose contrast with each other, and even *Allium cernuum,* though not flowering at this time, is encouraged in from the native woodland nearby. In another small rock area we are experimenting with a newly introduced group of Mexican *Phlox nana* and its hybrids.

Perennials abound on the south side of the house—the main border is perhaps fifty feet long, varying in width from eight to fifteen feet. We prepared the soil with 2 parts of local rocky soil mix to 3 parts of well-rotted organic material from a local stable, cultivated to a depth of twelve to fifteen inches; each summer we add a light two-inch mulch of similar organic material, which is worked in later in the year. Growth starts around the second week of April and by early May is up to three or four inches. At this time the necessary division and replanting is carried out. With the open soil, fairly heavy watering twice or three times a week keeps the plants moving. Early peonies and poppies bloom along with the Tall Bearded iris, and these are followed by a veritable array of traditionals such as delphinium, gypsophila, *Campanula persicifolia*, meadow rue, and the very bright Maltese cross.

Planting here is rather mixed, and with the condensed season—even on this side of the house perhaps only three months of real growth and flowers—some interesting combinations occur. In July a quite vigorous group of *Campanula glomerata* 'Superba' mixes with abandon against a background of *Lysimachia punctata*. Farther along much subtler tones appear, with the Colorado columbine, *Aquilegia caerulea*, overtopping an area of *Dianthus anatolicus* and *Achillea ageratifolia*. Later on in the season goldenrod dominates the background plantings and other members of the daisy family come into their glory. Ligularia catches the eye with its unusual leaf shape, especially *Ligularia dentata* 'Desdemona' and *L. przewalskii* 'The Rocket', and garden phlox and asters make splashes (the early varieties only, however, as the later ones, while growing prolifically, may not produce their buds early enough to avoid getting frosted—which can occur as early as the end of August some years).

A few plants of special interest are growing among the traditionals. *Malva alcea fastigiata*, with its pink flower spikes, blooms from mid-July until frost, and in the fall the bent white spikes of the gooseneck lysimachia, *Lysimachia clethroides*, contrast dramatically with a group of sunflowers. *Campanula persicifolia*, the peach bellflower, in both blue and white, has become so happy that it has naturalized and invaded the nearby clump of aspen trees, flourishing in the part shade. It also pops up in sundry other places. The aspens and pea trees (*Caragana fruticosa*) help to screen the southern boundary of the garden, filling in the area left vacant when several mature Ponderosa pines were killed by pine beetle some years ago.

To find one's way around the garden, one follows a set of gravel paths interspersed with a small series of steps made of old railroad ties, spaced to incorporate three- to four-inch planting areas between the treads. Thyme, *Veronica pectinata*, and pussytoes (*Antennaria parvifolia*) fill the spaces, making the risers easier to negotiate.

The feeling of intimacy is part of this small garden, which incorporates the natural surrounding landscape and plants and yet has many gems for the collector. It is maturing at a relatively fast pace, but nature will always be in charge, for the growing season will never be anything but limited. Fall foliage extends color a while longer, until the season of berries and leftover seed heads finally succumbs to the first heavy winter snow, which may arrive in October or early November.

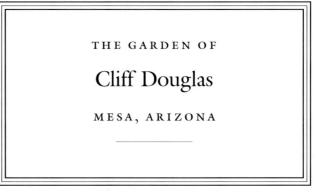
MY FONDNESS FOR PLANTS began when my mother, Dora Douglas, let me participate in her gardening activities. I was good with a shovel. During my childhood we moved numerous times, and planting a garden was always the first thing my mother did. The next occupants were assured of a vegetable garden, flower gardens, and shade trees. Roses were my mother's favorites, and her beautiful rose garden in Fresno, California, was her joy.

In 1982 my wife, Marilyn, and I purchased five acres on which to build a new home, later adding ten adjoining acres. The property, on the slope of Usery Mountain at an elevation of 1,850 feet, has a 220-degree view of the Valley of the Sun. The land was untouched Sonoran desert, covered with ironwood and palo verde trees, saguaro and barrel cactus, cholla, bur sage, creosote, brittle bush, jojoba, hedgehog, ocotillo, chuparosa, Mormon tea, catclaw acacia, wolfberry, prickly pear, and many other natives. (See the end of the essay for Latin names of these popular natives.)

We asked our son, John, an architect, to design the house, and landscape architect Steve Martino, a close family friend, to work with us in designing the garden. We could not have made better choices, for both showed great fondness for and sensitivity toward the incomparable richness and beauty of the Sonoran desert. The final result is a home totally appropriate to its site, set on a ridge between two washes, with the desert bumping gently up against its sides. The architecture and garden landscape seem always to have been a part of the natural setting.

The siting of the house and related structures took into account the priceless existing shrubs and trees, many of which were centuries old. Marilyn and I carefully saved and relocated all the ocotillos, hedgehogs, opuntias, and barrel cacti from various parts of the garden. We would often stand guard as large cement trucks came and went, to be sure they stayed on the drive and did not stray onto our beautiful desert. Marilyn was also busy designing and making terra-cotta tiles depicting desert birds and animals, and these we fixed on the masonry walls near entry points or gates throughout the garden. All of the scarred areas were then revegetated with indigenous plants, and closer in, other natives and plants from similar deserts of the world were added to the existing palette. It is now impossible to tell that any part of the property was ever disturbed.

In all, we planted seventy-four trees. Some were local or Arizona natives, such as blue, Sonoran, and Mexican palo verde, sweet acacia, desert willow, and western honey

Giant saguaros along the entry drive are surrounded with creosote and prickly pears. Two large Chilean mesquite trees shade the western walls of the house.

Acacia greggii   catclaw acacia

Acacia smallii   sweet acacia

Acacia stenophylla   shoestring acacia

Ambrosia deltoidea   bur sage

Carnegiea gigantea   saguaro cactus

Cercidium floridum   blue palo verde

Cercidium microphyllum   palo verde

Cercidium praecox   Sonoran palo verde

Chilopsis linearis   desert willow

Echinocereus spp.   hedgehog

Encelia farinosa   brittle bush

Ephedra trifurca   Mormon tea

Ferocactus wislizenii   barrel cactus

Fouquieria splendens   ocotillo

Geoffroea decorticans

   South American palo verde

Justicia californica   chuparosa

Larrea tridentata   creosote

Lycium fremontii   wolfberry

Olneya tesota   ironwood tree

Opuntia acanthocarpa   cholla

Opuntia phaeacantha   prickly pear

Parkinsonia aculeata

   Mexican palo verde

Prosopis alba   Argentine mesquite

Prosopis chilensis   Chilean mesquite

Prosopis juliflora var. *torreyana*

   western honey mesquite

Simmondsia chinensis   jojoba

Tecoma stans   Arizona yellow bell

In April, the late-evening sun lights up the bright red of the chuparosa (hummingbird) and the brilliant yellows of the brittle bush. Framing this flower show is a saguaro cactus, an ocotillo (buggy whip), and creosote. All of these plants are indigenous.

mesquite. Trees from other desert areas included Chilean and Argentine mesquite, South American palo verde, and shoestring acacia.

In front of the west-facing library window, a mesquite tree provides much-needed shade; under its branches a microclimate shelters understory plants. The seed pods of the mesquite are a favorite food of our many rock and antelope squirrels, and at night we sometimes turn on the lights under this tree to watch wild javelina gorging themselves. Just across from the entry, in front of another window, a desert willow and an Arizona yellow bell grow together, providing not only shade in summer but also, from March through October, a beautiful display of orchidlike flowers on the willow and yellow trumpets on the yellow bell. These two plants are a favorite of hummingbirds and verdins, and it is a rare occasion when these birds are not present.

Above: *Bougainvillea* 'Barbara Karst' provides summer color along a garden wall. In the foreground are an *Agave americana* and an Indian fig prickly pear.

Left: Near the entry, an Arizona yellow bell and orange bird of paradise, along with a potted bougainvillea, provide color throughout the summer and into fall. The yellow bell attracts verdins and hummingbirds.

Besides the trees, the most imposing plants in our garden are the giant saguaro, beautiful structures with arms extending upward. Less than a foot high when they are a few years old, these cacti grow to over thirty feet and live more than 150 years. In May and June they reward us with crowns of large white flowers. About the same time of year, the white-winged dove migrates up from Mexico, to stay on until the end of August, and in late June and July, along with a host of other birds, insects, and animals, they can eat their fill of the sweet watermelon-colored fruit.

To the south of the house, Harris' hawks have built a nest in a large saguaro. We have watched several hawk families be raised here—the young fledglings take their first flights up to the top of the saguaro's arms, then to the ground, and in stages up a nearby palo verde tree and back to the nest. The silhouette of the saguaros against the evening sunset and the city lights below is a sight we never tire of.

Near the garden walls, paths, and house walls, we added more than fifteen different species of prickly pear. With their sculptural shapes and shadows, these beautiful plants add great variety, contrast, and floral beauty to the garden. Their flowers, ranging from yellow through peach and pink to brilliant red-orange, appear from April to July, and their red fruit adds yet more color from June through August. The pads are of many different shapes, colors, and textures. *Opuntia violacea* has purple pads. *O. ficus-indica* grows upright to ten or twelve feet and appears in the garden against both house and garden walls, with the lower-growing varieties used throughout the planting beds and along walkways. Planted with the opuntias are several species of agave and the column-shaped *Stenocereus marginatus, S. thurberi*, and *Pachycereus schottii*.

For additional color, the garden has beds of red-flowered *Salvia greggii* from the Chihuahuan desert that bloom continuously throughout the year. A native perennial, *Penstemon parryi*, planted in beds and also interplanted, produces an incredible show during March and into April with its multiple stalks of three-foot flower spikes. Other penstemons included throughout the garden are the orange-flowered *P. superbus*, the lipstick-red *P. eatonii*, and the blue-lavender *P. spectabilis*.

Under the shade of a tree, *Justicia spicigera* shows its orange blossoms spring, summer,

Traditional garden flowers transformed by their desert setting: a spring show of lavender-flowered *Verbena gooddingii* and, in the rear, the tall pink spikes of *Penstemon parryi*. The penstemons are perennial and also spread from seed each year.

The strong, beautiful shapes and shadows of Indian fig prickly pears and shoestring acacia trees are reflected in the pool.

and fall, and for added summer color there are specimen plants of *Caesalpinia pulcherrima* (orange bird of paradise) and *Bougainvillea* 'Barbara Karst'. The bougainvilleas often frost back in the winter and take a considerable time to recover. There are also beds of *Verbena gooddingii* with blue-lavender blossoms; they burn out in summer and are removed, only to replace themselves each spring from seed. Both penstemons and verbenas are spreading down the washes, and when there is sufficient winter and spring rain, they become great wildflower displays. Interest and color come, too, from several different species of aloe and red yucca (*Hesperaloe parviflora*), both having waxy blossoms that seem to last for months.

Our plants are well adapted to the climate of this part of the Sonoran desert. The temperature falls to below freezing on the colder winter nights, and the daytime temperature exceeds 110° on the hottest days of summer. In June, July, and August it rises above 100° on most days. Annual rainfall averages about seven inches, falling during the winter and spring and during the monsoon season, from July to early September. Most of the garden takes care of itself, but closer to the house we give it some help during the summer by turning on drip-emitter systems and dragging a hose around. We are always happy when a summer thunderstorm produces enough rainfall to make the washes run and to store moisture that will keep the desert green for weeks and even months. Within five days after such a storm, a seemingly dead ocotillo will turn emerald-green with new leaves.

The spring show starts in late February. First the chuparosa flames with hundreds of trumpetlike red-orange flowers, and brittle bush starts to bloom bright yellow. In March the verbenas and penstemons add their color to the scene, along with the palo verde's spectacular yellow blossoms. It is at about this time that we see the first new families of Gambel's quail, with perhaps a dozen tiny babies in single file behind their parents. In April the tecoma flowers appear and the desert willows put forth their orchidlike blooms, lasting into November. The saguaros blossom, and the brilliant flowers of hedgehogs and prickly pears light up the desert until July. During the summer the ripe red fruits of saguaros and prickly pears add their color to that of the birds of paradise and bougainvillea. *Salvia greggii* continues in bloom throughout the year.

The joy of living here, of being a part of the Sonoran desert and its incredibly rich plant and animal life, is a privilege beyond compare. A good friend, Dr. Robert Breunig, director of the Desert Botanical Garden in Phoenix, once asked a Papago elder how he survived in the desert. The response was, "We do not survive here, we live here. This is our home." Marilyn and I know of what they speak. Nor do we survive here—this is our home. There is something beguiling about the Sonoran. I still have a fondness for formal gardens and for my mother's rose garden, but I have found nothing to compare with walking out into the backyard before sunrise to see the great horned owl looking at me from the top of the guesthouse and to hear the song of the curved-bill thrasher. We are fortunate indeed to have had the sensitivity of a Steve Martino to help us learn to appreciate the desert's natural beauty, and to have had both Steve and John to teach us that it is not necessary to destroy the desert in order to create a home within it.

The Gardeners

BENJAMIN BALDWIN, born in 1913, grew up in Alabama. He studied painting with Hans Hofmann, architecture at Princeton University, and town planning at Cranbrook Academy. After helping to establish the interior design section of Skidmore, Owings, and Merrill in New York City, he set up an independent practice in New York, Alabama, and Chicago, designing furniture and fabrics as well as buildings, including interiors and gardens. He now divides his time between East Hampton and Florida.

WILLIAM NATHANIEL BANKS grew up on his family's place, Bankshaven, where he continues to maintain the house and garden. His parents inspired his interest in gardening and landscape design. Since acquiring a late-eighteenth-century house in a New Hampshire village in 1965, he has also cultivated a much smaller garden and an apple orchard there. He has written numerous articles on old towns and historic houses and serves on the boards of museums, preservation groups, and historical societies in Georgia and New Hampshire.

CRAIG BERGMANN AND JAMES GRIGSBY own a prominent garden design and installation company in a suburb of Chicago. Craig Bergmann's training is in botany and biology. James Grigsby is a former art professor.

FRANK CABOT, born in 1925, devotes most of his time, now that he is retired, to gardening in Cold Spring, New York, and in La Malbaie, Quebec. Both gardens are large and diverse, but they are quite different. His special interests are alpines and woodland plants and the design and development of new gardens. Currently he is at work launching The Garden Conservancy, an organization whose purpose is to "encourage and facilitate the transition of exceptional North American private gardens to public status and thereby preserve them for posterity."

CHARLES O. CRESSON was born in 1954 and has lived at Hedgleigh Spring since he was five years old. His early interest in gardening led to a B.A. in ornamental horticulture from the University of Vermont, which included studies at Bath University in England. He has worked at the Royal Horticultural Society's Wisley Garden, the Kalmthout Arboretum in Belgium, and Longwood Gardens, as well as with Liddon Pennock at Meadowbrook Farm. He is a co-author, with Jeff Ball, of *The 60-Minute Flower Garden* and is working on a book about the design and care of American flower gardens.

ROBERT DASH lives and paints and writes in Sagaponack, New York.

HENRY CLIFTON DOUGLAS, born in 1930 on a cotton farm near Yuma, Arizona, grows cotton and has a tree nursery in Queen Creek. He is married to Marilyn Plummer, and they have three children. When he is not busy farming, he gardens, plays tennis and a peculiar game of golf, and currently serves as president of the board of trustees of the Desert Botanical Garden in Phoenix.

JOSEPH ECK AND WAYNE WINTERROWD, partners in North Hill, the garden design firm they founded in 1977, also created the garden of the same name. Joe Eck, born near Philadelphia in 1945, earned a degree in philosophy and then taught English and Latin in public high schools in southern Vermont. He travels throughout the northeastern United States as a garden design consultant. Wayne Winterrowd, born in 1941 in Shreveport, Louisiana, taught for twenty-three years and then retired to devote himself full-time to garden design and gardening. He is a frequent contributor to *Horticulture* magazine.

HAROLD EPSTEIN was born in 1902 in New York City, where he resided for thirty years before moving to Westchester County. He and his wife, Esta, have two daughters. A graduate of New York University, he is a certified public accountant and had a varied business career. Since his retirement, at sixty, he has devoted his time to many aspects of horticulture and related world travel. He has been active in many specialized horticultural organizations, with a policy of not permitting business interests to interfere with his hobbies.

JOHN GASTON FAIREY, born in 1930, grew up on a farm near the small town of St. Matthews, South Carolina. After pursuing liberal arts at Erskine College, he studied painting at the Pennsylvania Academy of the Fine Arts and received an M.F.A. from the University of Pennsylvania. For twenty-six years he has taught a design studio in the College of Architecture at Texas A&M University, where he has received awards for innovative and distinguished teaching.

WILLIAM H. FREDERICK, JR., born in 1926, has gardened since the age of eight; Ashland Hollow is his third garden. A registered landscape architect specializing in residential garden design, he is a member of the board of Callaway Gardens and a past president and member of the board of Longwood Gardens. He is the author of *100 Great Garden Plants* and is now completing a book on plant combinations for American gardens.

RYAN GAINEY, a native of Hartsville, South Carolina, was born in 1944 and studied ornamental horticulture at Clemson University. He is co-owner of The Potted Plant, The Cottage Garden, and The Connoisseurs' Garden in Atlanta and is a garden designer with projects in the eastern United States and in France. He lectures extensively on his own garden and on aspects of gardening in the South and serves on the advisory board of the Atlanta Flower Show.

JIMMY GRAHAM was born in Union Springs, Alabama, in 1937. In 1962 he moved to Memphis, where he now has his own interior design firm. He and his wife, Mary Ann, have one son.

ROBERT W. GRIMES, a product of UCLA, spent three years in the military service in China during World War II. For ten years he was a geologist in South America and for twenty years a contractor with his family business. Now retired, he has until recently had one foot in Brazil, but is resident in Los Angeles.

HARLAND J. HAND, born in Minnesota in 1922, started his first garden when he was eight. In 1948 he moved to California and began a career in teaching. He started his present garden in 1955 and designed and built his home eleven years later. A contributor to *Pacific Horticulture* magazine, he has served as executive vice president of the Pacific Horticulture Foundation and as president of the California Horticultural Society and is now on the board of directors of the Friends of The University of California Botanical Garden in Berkeley. Since his retirement, in 1982, he has been designing gardens.

RON JOHNSON AND GEORGE SCHOELLKOPF have been gardening in northwestern Connecticut for the past decade. Ron Johnson, born in 1945, studied landscape architecture and painting at Cornell University, to which he returned briefly to teach drawing after earning his degree. He then founded a company that developed and manufactured textile products for such diverse institutions as Lord and Taylor, the Metropolitan Museum, and the Museum of Natural History. Over the years he has found time to design gardens for friends and clients and has recently resumed a career as a landscape painter. George Schoellkopf, born in 1942 in Dallas, was educated at Yale University. After a short stint as a novice in a Benedictine monastery, he earned an M.A. in art history from Columbia University, and then began to deal in eighteenth-century American furniture and folk art, soon opening his gallery on Madison Avenue. He is a founding member of a committee devoted to the restoration and completion of the garden designed by Gertrude Jekyll for the Glebe House in Woodbury, Connecticut, and is also on the board of the newly formed Garden Conservancy.

ALBERT RICHARD LAMB III, born in New York City in 1943, is a landscape architect with an international design practice. After studying landscape architecture at the Rhode Island School of Design and the University of Michigan, he was awarded a fellowship at the American Academy in Rome, which enabled him to travel widely in Europe, Scandinavia, and the Middle East. He has taught at Harvard University, is on the faculty of the Massachusetts Institute of Technology, and has guest-lectured on design at universities in America and Sweden.

CARL NEELS, born in 1939 in Baltimore, graduated from the University of Maryland with a degree in horticulture. As an army officer he was able to travel to and learn about plants and garden design in many parts of the world, and his travels were enhanced when he became a diplomatic courier with the State Department and then a sales manager with Pan American Airways. In 1984 he formed a landscape design company, to which he now devotes all of his efforts.

KEVIN MICHAEL NICOLAY was born in 1957 and raised mainly in Ohio. At a tender age he went out into the garden, and with the exception of time spent in school in Cleveland and New York, he has been there ever since. One of the most accomplished botanical illustrators working today, he divides his time between painting, writing and talking about, and growing too many plants.

MARSHALL OLBRICH was born in Madison, Wisconsin, in 1920. After receiving an M.A. in comparative literature from the University of Wisconsin, he spent six years desultorily pursuing graduate studies at Berkeley in philosophy. After spending a few enjoyable years in San Francisco, he moved to the country in 1959 with his friend Lester Hawkins; together they started a garden that has remained an all-consuming project to this day.

J. LIDDON PENNOCK, JR., born in 1913, occupies a number of positions in the vortex of horticultural life in the Philadelphia area. He is a past president of the Pennsylvania Horticultural Society and a member of the advisory and landscape committees of Longwood Gardens, and serves also on the advisory boards of the Morris Arboretum and the Ladew Topiary Gardens. He is president of and permanent advisor to the Philadelphia Flower Show and a trustee of the Delaware Valley College of Science and Agriculture.

ANDREW PIERCE, who was born in England in 1935, came to America in 1976. Holder of Britain's National Diploma in Horticulture, he is now the assistant director of the Denver Botanic Gardens. With his wife he hikes in the Rockies admiring the alpine plants, some of which he grows in his own garden. His occupations as a lecturer, past president of the Colorado Garden and Home Show, and director of the Vail Alpine Garden take him to all parts of the state. His other interests are conservation and the hardiness of perennials at high elevations.

GEORGE IRVINE RADFORD was born in Canada in 1931. Half Irish and half English, he spent his childhood largely in Northern Ireland, where his Irish grandmother inspired him with her love of gardens. After moving to Vancouver with his family, he studied ornamental horticulture under Dr. John Neill at the University of British Columbia. He then settled in Victoria, where from 1973 until his recent retirement he was employed by a municipal parks department. A past president of the Victoria Horticultural Society, he is now an executive member and the garden notes editor.

ANTHONY SANTASIERO was born in Westchester, New York, in 1949 and discovered his love for gardening at an early age. He studied at the State University at Buffalo and in 1979 moved to New York City, where he started in the field of interior design; he now owns and operates a firm in Manhattan.

CECIL SMITH received a degree in business from Oregon State University. Until his retirement he was a farmer, growing grass seed. He is a charter member of the Rhododendron Species Foundation and of the American Rhododendron Society, whose Pioneer Award he has received, in addition to bronze and gold medals for his articles in the society's journals and for his contributions of photographs, pollen, cuttings, and seed. He is married to Molly Beatty, and they have two sons.

MARCO POLO STUFANO, born in 1939, grew up in Queens, New York, where he tended a vegetable plot with his father next to the tracks of the Long Island Railroad. He graduated from Brown University with a degree in fine arts. His career in horticulture was launched when he worked at the New York Botanical Garden under Thomas H. Everett, who recommended him as director of horticulture at Wave Hill. He is its first and only director.

PHILLIP WATSON, born in Lexington, Mississippi, in 1952, gained a B.S. in horticulture from Mississippi State University. Since 1982 he has owned Washington Gardens in Fredericksburg, Virginia, and has worked as a garden designer for clients from Florida to Manhattan. He also lectures on a wide variety of gardening topics.

Photograph Credits

Photographs not otherwise credited are by the garden owner.

Title page: Gottlieb Hampfler
Foreword: p. vii, Richard Brown
Introduction: p. x, Gottlieb Hampfler; p. 2, Derek Fell; p. 3, Historic Annapolis, Richard Moxley;
p. 4, Terry Richardson, Courtesy Middleton Place; p. 5, Derek Fell;
pp. 6, 7, 8, Arthur Sylvester; p. 9, Michael McKinley; p. 11, Gottlieb Hampfler
The Gardens: pp. 12–13, David Schilling
William Banks: pp. 14, 16, 18, 21, Richard Moore, Courtesy *Gardens of Georgia*
(Peachtree Publishers); pp. 15, 17, 19, 20, Deloye Burrell
Liddon Pennock: Gottlieb Hampfler
Frank Cabot: pp. 36, 39–43, Mick Hales
Joseph Eck and Wayne Winterrowd: pp. 44–48, Richard Brown; p. 49, Joseph Eck
Marshall Olbrich: Lester Hawkins
Ron Johnson and George Schoellkopf: George Schoellkopf
Charles Cresson: p. 63, Liz Ball; pp. 65–67, Richard Brown
Cecil Smith: pp. 78–80 top, Jerry Pavia; pp. 80 bottom, 81, Joanne Pavia
Harold Epstein: Michael McKinley
John Fairey: pp. 89–91, C. Schoenfield; pp. 92 top, 93, © Julie Ryan; p. 92 bottom, M. Uhrbrock
Robert Grimes: pp. 94, 96, 97, © Kathlene Persoff; p. 95, Dick Rosmini
Anthony Santasiero: Curtice Taylor
Craig Bergmann and James Grigsby: Judith Bromley
Jimmy Graham: Allen Mims
Ryan Gainey: David Schilling
Harland Hand: p. 130, Joanne Pavia; pp. 131–134, Jerry Pavia; p. 135, Jerry Harpur
Robert Dash: p. 137, Mick Hales
William Frederick: pp. 142, 143, 145 right, 146, Larry Albee; p. 145 left, Gottlieb Hampfler; p. 147, Jerry Harpur
Benjamin Baldwin: p. 149, Mick Hales
Andrew Pierce: Rita Buchanan, Courtesy *Fine Gardening*
(some first appeared in *Fine Gardening*, March/April 1989, pp. 40–45)
Cliff Douglas: pp. 158, 160, 161, 163, © Christine Keith; p. 162, Richard Maack

DESIGNED BY SUSAN MARSH

COPYEDITED BY DOROTHY STRAIGHT

PRODUCTION COORDINATED BY CHRISTINA HOLZ ECKERSON

COMPOSITION BY DEKR CORPORATION

PRINTED AND BOUND BY TIEN WAH PRESS